# THE DIGITAL EXECUTIVE

A Guide for Tech and Non-Tech Leaders

Creating Innovative & Resilient Organizations
in the Age of AI and Digital

## CHRISTOPHER MARTLEW

The manufacturer's authorised representative in the EU for product safety is Authorised Rep Compliance Ltd,
71 Lower Baggot Street, Dublin D02 P593 Ireland
(www.arccompliance.com)

Troubador Publishing Ltd
Unit E2 Airfield Business Park,
Harrison Road, Market Harborough,
Leicestershire. LE16 7UL
Tel: 0116 2792299
Email: books@troubador.co.uk
Web: www.troubador.co.uk


ISBN 978 1836281 177


British Library Cataloguing in Publication Data.
A catalogue record for this book is available from the British Library.


Typeset in 11pt Gill Sans by Troubador Publishing Ltd, Leicester, UK

For Kate Mae,
who will look back and smile

# ACCLAIM FOR
# *THE DIGITAL EXECUTIVE*

Chris Martlew masterfully unpacks the complex dynamics of technology-driven change. *The Digital Executive* provides a simple and pragmatic framework for leaders to reimagine their roles and embrace the challenges that AI and digital transformation bring.

Highly recommended for all who are navigating the complexities of modern technology. Chris leverages his vast experience as a world-class tech leader with an engaging and accessible writing style that makes this an inspiring read for leaders. If you are looking for a navigation aid to help you steer through the tsunami of technologies disrupting our world, you won't find a more useful resource.

**Brian Bacon,**
**Founder and Executive Chairman, Oxford Leadership Group**

The rapid evolution of AI is shortening the shelf life of previously effective strategic choices. Leaders face the crucial task of reconfiguring their businesses across technological, organizational, and human dimensions to address the vast impact of the combined forces of data, digital, and AI. This book offers valuable insights for anyone preparing to lead their organization through the tectonic AI shift, where augmented intelligence will become the norm. An essential read for all executives.

**Vikas K. Verma,**
**CEO and President of Engineering, Zimetrics**

With a keen understanding of the intricate dance between technology and human behaviour, Chris Martlew masterfully dissects the complexities of AI and digital transformation. His insights resonate with a practical wisdom that transcends buzzwords, providing leaders with a clear path towards innovation and resilience. This book is more than a guide; it's a manifesto for those ready to embrace the future with courage and agility. Martlew's focus on the human element makes this an essential read for any leader committed to creating a vibrant, adaptable organization.

**Dr. Leandro Herrero,**
**Chief Organization Architect and CEO, The Chalfont Project Ltd**

Crafted with a practitioner's eye, Chris Martlew's new book serves as a strategic guide for business leaders, addressing the essential role of technology in our contemporary digital age. Very readable and packed with jargon-busting clarifications, insights and wisdom.

**Martin Ward, West Midlands Tech Commissioner**

Chris Martlew's people-centric perspective on the role of the digital executive is especially relevant in an era of rapid change and uncertainty about the future of work. This book unpacks the underlying concepts of a contemporary techno-social architecture, with a particular focus on integrating emerging AI capabilities. In doing so, Chris Martlew recasts the digital executive beyond the individual, toward a 'distributed persona'. One that every executive should adopt.

**Ivan Sean, Global Advisor, AI & Emerging Technologies,**
**Alumnus, Institute for the Future**

As CIO of De Nederlandsche Bank, I'm deeply involved in the challenges of AI, digital transformation, regulatory compliance, and cybersecurity. Chris Martlew's *The Digital Executive* is a valuable guide that addresses these challenges with precision and clarity. The book's insights into AI and cloud computing provide a strategic framework that is particularly relevant to the banking sector, where data security and operational efficiency are paramount. For any executive in banking, this book is not only a recommendation – it's a great read.

**Arjen de Graaf, CIO, De Nederlandsche Bank (DNB)**

Chris Martlew's new book turns complex tech topics into an engaging read. It's like having a smart friend explain AI and digital transformation over coffee. Enjoyable, eye-opening, and essential for today's leaders.

**Frits Steenmeijer,**
**Associate Partner, Connective Payments**

In an ever-changing world, this is a hitch-hikers guide for today's digital leaders. Make sure to strap-in, it may be a bumpy ride ahead.

**Nicolas Castellon, Director,**
**Cybersecurity Services Europe, Sygnia**

As the CEO of a company dedicated to delivering 24/7, fully resilient IT services, I found The Digital Executive to be an inspiring read. Chris Martlew's exploration of cloud computing, cybersecurity, and AI offers practical approaches for enhancing system resilience and operational efficiency. His insights into creating agile, fusion organizations are particularly valuable in our line of work, where uptime and reliability are non-negotiable. For leaders in the IT infrastructure space, *The Digital Executive* provides an essential playbook for navigating today's digital challenges with confidence and foresight.

**Frans Ter Borg, CEO & Founder, Quanza**

Organizations must continuously adapt and act in response to the rapidly changing world we live in. AI represents one of the most significant changes, often challenging for organizations to fully grasp. This book provides leaders with the foundational knowledge and insights to be better prepared for this new transformation.

**Bob Voermans, Founder, LoopingOne**

Applying his deep experience, Chris Martlew breaks down complex topics such as AI, cloud technology, architecture and cybersecurity into understandable, actionable steps, providing the tools and strategies needed to successfully transform an organization. *The Digital Executive* deserves sanctuary on the bookshelves of all those ready to lead the digital revolution.

**Padraig O'Riordain, CISO and Founder of Emerald Hill IT**

Captivatingly written, *The Digital Executive* is a must-read for business leaders grappling with the fascinating advances in AI and all its implications. It offers invaluable insights into the technologies and processes that are shaping all of our futures today.

**Jeroen Berkhout, Literary Author**

With a context of increasing cybersecurity risks and the decentralization of tech roles, this book offers practical guidance on how compliance and governance can evolve to meet these challenges. Chris Martlew's style is professional yet engaging, making it easy for business leaders, including those with non-technical backgrounds, to grasp the content.

**Tamara Berben, Chief Compliance Officer**

*The Digital Executive* offers critical insights for today's leaders, addressing the complex tech and organizational challenges they face. It underscores the urgent need to rethink strategies and adapt in the rapidly evolving landscape of AI and digital transformation. Having spent most of my career as a business leader in cyber, risk & compliance, the Cybersecurity chapter is more than just a resource – it articulates a fundamental piece of the puzzle. Authored by someone who has "walked the talk", this book will enlighten in a fresh, compelling, and thought-provoking way. An essential read.

**Joseph Souren, Founder, SIGMA Consulting**

*The Digital Executive* underscores the essential role of digital capabilities in modern organizations, highlighting the need for digital literacy at every level. As IT and operational technology converge, this book explores how AI and other innovations are driving business growth and revolutionizing operations. It offers valuable insights into aligning leadership with digital transformation to secure a competitive advantage in the future. Thoroughly recommended!

**Mark Jesse, Founder and Partner, Chiaro Group**

Having enjoyed Chris Martlew's previous works, I found this book particularly impactful. It dives deeply into how AI and digital technologies are revolutionizing leadership and organizational strategies. What sets this book apart is its practical approach to integrating these innovations into everyday leadership. I would highly recommend my clients to buy this book and I'm confident it will inspire and benefit them in their leadership responsibilities—even better, I'd be excited to offer them a copy!

**Bart Bossers, Commercial Director, INISI ICT**

*The Digital Executive* by Chris Martlew is a great read for leaders ready to embrace the AI revolution while facing the challenges of digital transformation. The book offers invaluable insights for executives across all industries. Engaging and insightful. Highly recommended.

**Olav Pannenborg, CEO, Supply Chain Group**

*The Digital Executive* is the right book at the right time for any executive looking to shape the future with the help of technology. Chris Martlew doesn't just explain this technological revolution; he hands you the map and compass to succeed in it. Whether you're a seasoned IT leader or an executive from a non-technical background, this book meets you where you are. A recommended read and a call to action!

**Juan Manuel Gómez Ramos,**
**Lean-Agile and Change Management Consultant**

# CONTENTS

# FOREWORD

In the swift currents of technological innovation, artificial intelligence and digital transformation have become undeniably central to every aspect of our society. As you embark on reading *The Digital Executive*, you engage with the essential dynamics that define our era.

Throughout my career, across multiple continents and industries, I've observed the profound impact that digital technology can have – not just economically, but culturally and socially. We are in the early days of a revolution powered by AI, where machines that learn and think can potentially redefine what it means to live and work. This isn't just about automation or mechanical efficiency; it's about the potential for AI to enhance our human capacities and to solve problems on scales we've never before managed. As such, this book doesn't just prepare you to implement new technologies – it challenges you to rethink how those technologies can influence human organizational structures and outcomes.

AI's implications for digital transformation are vast. It empowers organizations to break free from traditional constraints of space and time, connecting global teams instantly and enabling them to operate more synchronously. As businesses transform, so do societies. The integration of AI into various sectors – from healthcare, improving patient outcomes, through data-driven insights, to education and personalized learning experiences – illustrates the potential for AI to enhance the quality of life universally.

The impact of digital transformation is profound – altering the very fabric of how businesses operate and compete. It has the power to democratize information, streamline processes, and unlock new opportunities in markets previously inaccessible. Yet, as we integrate these technologies deeper into the sinews of our corporations, the responsibility to wield them wisely grows exponentially. This evolution is not without its challenges; the path is fraught with complexity, requiring a nuanced understanding of both the capabilities of new technologies and the ethical considerations they entail.

With great power comes great responsibility. The rapid deployment of digital technologies and AI raises critical ethical questions about privacy, security, how we organize our businesses and our society, and the future of employment. It is crucial that as leaders, we not only embrace these technologies but also actively participate in shaping the policies and ethical frameworks that govern their use. This book aims to equip you with the foresight and knowledge to navigate these complex issues.

Reflecting on the accelerating pace of change, I often recall the projects and meetings across global organizations where the balance between speed and caution was critical. The similar experiences and research documented in these pages are designed to provide strategic insights that balance innovation with integrity, helping you to lead not just effectively but wisely.

As we look to the future, the integration of AI in business and society promises a new era of innovation. *The Digital Executive* is an excellent guide through this uncharted terrain, ensuring you are ready to lead in an age where change is the only constant and where technology, wisely applied, is the most powerful tool for building a resilient, thriving future.

Chris Martlew reflects a positive, confident, yet prudent perspective on the future of our organizations shaped by artificial intelligence. The narrative embodies a belief in technology's capacity to improve both society and business, with a pragmatic approach filled with optimism and insight. As we venture into this exhilarating era, we need to engage enthusiastically with the transformative power of technology in our organizations, envisioning a future where we are enriched and enlivened by these amazing ideas.

**Michael Tobin, OBE**
Founder and Executive Chairman, Tobin Ventures Ltd

# PREFACE

Looking back through human history, we can be proud of our remarkable achievements – from the invention of the wheel to space travel, quantum mechanics, artificial intelligence and augmented reality. These things showcase humankind's incredible creativity, ingenuity and relentless pursuit of progress.

Many new technologies present both opportunities and threats – AI falls unquestionably into both categories. Technology is about rapid change; just as we're getting used to the last *big thing*, the next *big thing* comes crashing onto our consciousness. AI is already impacting much of how we live, work, and play. AGI (artificial **general** intelligence or human-like intelligence) will be the greatest and most sudden evolution of intelligence on our planet since *Homo sapiens.*

Change is a choice. In Darwinian and economic terms, organizations must change now, change soon, or die slowly. Some choose slow death by default – by not deciding to embrace innovative technologies and new ways of working. Others struggle with transformation or fall at the first hurdle. Many are still stuck in waterfall software development, with old technology, weak cybersecurity and desperately slow change cultures. Others succeed in grasping the opportunities that tech offers and are propelled into success, fame, and fortune. And, one hopes, into making our world a better place along the way.

We don't just want change – we want it to be successful; we want it to stick; and we want it to prepare us for the next change. In digital transformation, the winners will be those who adopt bold, well-integrated digital strategies. The greatest rewards will go to the early adopters, with fast followers who excel in operational efficiency also finding significant success.[1] Others may be too late.

It's important to distinguish between digital transformation and artificial intelligence, as they can be conflated but represent two distinct concepts. Digital transformation refers to the wholesale integration of digital technologies into all areas of a business, fundamentally changing how organizations operate and deliver value to customers.

AI, on the other hand, is a specific set of technologies that enable machines to learn from data and perform tasks that typically would require human intelligence.

Where many books treat these topics separately, this book integrates them, reflecting how AI is a critical driver of digital transformation rather than an afterthought. By weaving AI into the broader narrative of digital transformation, the book aims to provide an inclusive guide for leaders to navigate the complexities of the digital age effectively and strategically.

My first book (in 2004)[2] examined the characteristics of what I called an *agile organization* and an *agile leader*. The agile approach made sense and suggested a route to improving organizational life and business performance – not only in IT and software engineering but more broadly in the architecture of our organizations.

We use the word *transformation* to indicate a level of deep change required to engage with, and master, the challenges that digital technology brings. My second book (in 2015)[3] explored the transformation required to meet the challenges of our time with confidence. It was about deep change, about changing the "mind" of an organization and building agile teams to support meaningful and lasting business transformation.

Fast forward… and agile, with its younger sibling DevOps, now forms the dominant organizational paradigm not only for software development, but also for other business processes.

*The Digital Executive* builds on the concepts of business agility and deep change to explore an approach for understanding digital and AI transformation and for architecting organizations where IT – and AI – are completely embedded into the strategy and structure of the business.

This book is intended to be a guide for tech and non-tech leaders. By "non-tech", I mean anyone who hasn't necessarily been trained in computer science, IT or AI, but may now be stepping into the role of a "digital executive", overseeing the technology-related aspects of their organization. I've therefore aimed to provide sufficient technical detail to ensure an understanding of what's going on, without overwhelming with IT jargon, acronyms, and abbreviations. I've included a selection of tech terms in the appendix.

# It's Hard to Know Exactly What Happens Next

*What happens when you're in a meeting and your AI team member disagrees with a critical decision you're taking?*

*What happens when you have two autonomous AI agents talking to each other, and they start to speak their own language?*

*What happens when the most popular programming language on Earth is English?*

*What happens when AI language translation enables real-time conversation across all languages?*

*What happens when we fully integrate AI with a digital transformation strategy?*

And countless similar questions. We don't have all the answers; nevertheless, it's up to us to be prepared.

One thing is certain: not much of the future will be a linear extrapolation of the past. We must determine our own paths through uncertainty and ambiguity and make new footprints in the sands of time.

# How This Book Is Structured

The book is structured into seven parts across twelve chapters. The main chapters close with a brief summary and five bullet points for consideration and/or action. While it can be dipped into, I'd recommend reading it in sequence to follow the train of thought.

## Chapter Breakdown:

- **Introduction:** Opportunities, threats, Conway's Law and fusion organizations. *Chapter one.*

- **Technology:** The forces that are driving and empowering this transformation – including AI, cloud, APIs, big data and the internet of things. *Chapters two to four.*

- **Organizational Transformation:** The changes in the senior leadership team, the "digital executive", and, more specifically, the changing roles of the CEO, CIO and CTO. *Chapters five to six.*

- **Software, Product, and Architecture:** The AI opportunity and how to apply agile and DevOps structures, models, and architectures to create flexible and resilient organizations. *Chapters seven to nine.*

- **Cybersecurity, Risk, and Compliance:** Don't hit the headlines! Rethinking security for transformation and AI. *Chapter ten.*

- **Leadership and People:** A recurring theme throughout the book, but I wanted to conclude with this aspect of the changes ahead. It may be a bumpy ride. *Chapter eleven.*

- **Wrapping Up:** Back to Conway's Law. Where do we go from here? *Chapter twelve.*

# CHAPTER 1

# A Captivating Promise

## Foundations for Success with AI and Digital

*The future is not inevitable. We can influence it, if we know what we want it to be.*
*~ Charles Handy*

*The future with AI and humans interacting will be a harmonious blend of technology and humanity, enhancing our lives and unlocking unprecedented potential.*
*~ ChatGPT-4o*

*Longevity in this business is about being able to reinvent yourself or invent the future.*
*~ Satya Nadella*

# Five Observations

This book is built around five observations:

1. How we interact with technology is reshaping our daily lives, transforming the way we live, work, and play at an astonishing pace. It's not just change, it's a revolution happening in real time.
2. Organizations must undertake a fundamental recalibration in response to the rise of digital capabilities and artificial intelligence. This requires a profound rethinking of operational, organizational, and strategic foundations.
3. Digital transformation and artificial intelligence are not projects with end points but long-term programs that need to be deeply integrated into every aspect of organizational life.
4. Information technology is too important to be left up to the IT department.* The future calls for what we might term "fusion organizations" – environments where IT is seamlessly integrated into every department and function. This approach decentralizes IT, making it a shared responsibility that permeates every aspect of the organization.
5. In fusion organizations, the role of the executive also undergoes transformation. All executives, regardless of their traditional domain, become "digital executives", driving the integration of digital capabilities throughout their spheres of influence. It's a shift that promises to redefine leadership for the coming decades.

We're navigating a time of significant upheaval: from political and economic shifts to societal changes and, unquestionably, technological innovations. It's a time of rapid learning and growth, putting us right at the end of a hockey stick curve, as it were.

---

\* A tip of the hat to David Packard, co-founder of HP, who famously said that marketing was too important to be left up to the marketing department.

# Opportunities and Threats

AI doesn't just improve efficiency; it has the same fundamental ability that the Industrial Revolution had to accelerate the pace of change. In the Industrial Revolution, machines didn't just replace human labour to manufacture products, they also manufactured other machines.

Moore's Law is legendary but is losing its relevance. Coined by the co-founder of Intel, the law posits that the transistor density of chips will double approximately every eighteen months. While still holding true to some extent, its significance has waned in the face of emerging hardware and software architectures. Cloud computing, ultra-high-density chip designs, and advances in artificial intelligence – both in hardware and software – are now the primary drivers of exponential technology growth.

Functionality delivered previously by dedicated hardware boxes is now programmed in software running somewhere in a cloud data centre. The term "hardware" has almost become a misnomer, and entire systems are programmed onto chips with tens of billions of transistors. These chips feed the insatiable appetite for power required by modern applications.

The opportunities are there in front of us, but so are the threats. Cybercrime is growing exponentially. The archetypical fourteen-year-old kid hacking websites from their bedroom is now a lot less likely to succeed. However, nation states and terrorist organizations with deep pockets, patience, persistence, and supported by AI are posing a greater threat than ever.

AI is a captivating promise that is already delivering results and, as always with new tech, a fair amount of disruption. AI in turn accelerates other industries that apply its algorithms to create new drugs, provide better customer service, catch fraudsters, trade stocks, and so on. Applying digital technology in general, and AI specifically, will enable firms to aim for both customer intimacy and operational excellence – the conventional trade-offs no longer apply. Technology can make humans more efficient, while humans can add value by being flexible, communicative, and empathetic.

AI can provide a competitive edge in an increasingly digital marketplace. AI-driven insights lead to better strategic decisions, while automation frees up human resources for more creative and complex tasks. As AI technology advances, its applications will expand, making it essential for businesses to adopt AI to remain relevant and competitive. Ignoring AI means risking falling behind in a world where agility, efficiency, and data-driven strategies are paramount.

With so many moving parts, putting a high level of granularity into strategic thinking becomes increasingly moot. Strategy is steadily becoming more emergent than deliberate, driven by the rapid developments in AI and the accelerating pace of digital transformation. Traditional strategic planning, characterized by long-term, deliberate, and often rigid frameworks, is being complemented, if not replaced, by more dynamic and adaptable approaches. Organizations need a strong sense of purpose and a well-architected structure with "just enough" strategy.

The reality facing business leaders now is how to create organization structures and processes that allow firms to move at speed within the guard rails of a strong enterprise purpose, a resilient organization structure, and a long-term plan. The chapters that follow aim to support this process of crafting "just enough" strategy.

The evolving response to the AI and digital challenge is to distribute tech responsibility and capability across the organization. To embed IT deeply into every discipline, every team, every part of the organization. To make every executive a "digital executive".

Achieving this distributed autonomy means that leaders in every discipline need to be equipped with a sufficient level of understanding of how tech works and how tech leaders think. As McKinsey[4] puts it, "Understanding technology is now a core skill required of every business leader." Whether you're in marketing, sales, finance, operations, customer service, or any other area of business… you're also in IT.

Is this new? Well, yes and no. It's always made sense – indeed, it's a requirement – for executives to have some sense of how finance works. In a typical MBA syllabus, finance will take up the bulk of the learning for many students. Some understanding of a balance sheet, P&L, and cash flow is a rudimentary requirement. The vocabulary of assets, liabilities, costs, revenues, margins, and earnings (before or after interest, taxes, depreciation, amortization) is well established.

However, accounting has been around for hundreds of years (Italian Luca Pacioli wrote his treatise on double-entry bookkeeping in 1494) and we've had time to understand, adapt, and use (and misuse) its protocols.

Compare and contrast with information technology that has only been around for, let's say, fifty years. Since the dawn of the PC, the microchip, and the BASIC programming language, we've all got at least a rudimentary understanding of how computers work. But the vocabulary is not as stable as it is in finance with technology changing at jaw-dropping speed. These tech changes are not just about chips, fibre-optic cables and clever bits of software; they are organizational and epic in their impact.

The advent of agile organization structures, cloud computing and AI is democratizing IT across organizations. All disciplines now have access to incredible powers to transform the way they operate and cooperate. AI is also driving fusion organization structures by enabling the decentralization and democratization of technology decision-making and implementation. As AI becomes more accessible and user-friendly, IT teams shift from centralized control to a more collaborative and distributed model, where business units and domain experts play a greater role in driving AI adoption and innovation.

# Conway's Law and Fusion Organizations

From a technology perspective, loosely coupled architectures, AI and cloud capabilities are helping to address the challenges. But what about the organization?

Conway's Law[5] is a great adage in IT systems development: "Any organization that designs a system will produce a design whose structure is a copy of the organization's communication structure." In other words, all the hierarchies, politics, social networks, ecosystems, power structures, committees, processes, and gaps in an organization will be reflected in its IT systems. For better and for worse.

The principle suggests that the architecture of IT systems is inherently linked to the social dynamics and communication patterns within an organization. As such, to achieve a seamless fusion of technology and business, we need to move beyond thinking of entities like IT and business as separate parts of the organization. Instead, we should view the organization as a cohesive whole where all parts are interrelated and intraconnected. This holistic approach recognizes that the relationships within entities are just as important as those between them.

To transcend traditional limitations, organizations must dramatically rethink and adapt their structures and roles. This means elevating positions like the enterprise architect and chief technology officer to central roles that drive innovation and integration across all functions. By embracing the idea of fusion, where technology and business strategies are intrinsically and explicitly linked, organizations can cultivate an environment where innovation thrives, and efficiency is maximized. This holistic perspective not only aligns with Conway's Law but also ensures that every facet of the organization contributes to its overall success and agility in the digital age.

Agility has become so embedded in the way we do business that it is no longer the exciting organizational topic that it once was.[6] However, flexibility in organizational structures is more important than ever. Agile boards, agile governance, agile engineering and operations... agile is ubiquitous. We are seeing autonomous, small-scale, orchestrated systems and teams across the enterprise. For the IT folks, this may seem like Conway's Law in reverse: akin to applying the architectural principles of application programming interfaces (APIs), cloud and microservices to human organization design.

Yet this is an incredibly important organizational evolution (as we shall discover in greater detail later) because it narrows the distance between what an organization wants and what its technology teams are capable of delivering. We become less constrained by the limits of technology. The vocabulary merges. The conversations are more fluid. There is greater understanding and empathy. More trust. Less "them and us" between the business and tech communities.

Glance at any team in a fusion organization and it's hard to see who is a technology-side engineer and who is on the business side – in fact there are no sides, and it doesn't really matter as long as it works. McKinsey refers to the agile work areas as "domains"[7]: units of organization that control "every step in fulfilling their function, from beginning to end". Whatever the nomenclature, the mission is to decentralize, democratize, and embed IT.

Time is of the essence and, to some extent, we all need to "blitzscale"[8] – in Reid Hoffman's words – prioritizing speed over efficiency in uncertain times. This approach involves rapidly scaling up a company's operations, even if it means sacrificing some efficiency in the short term. By focusing on growth and agility, companies can seize new opportunities and stay ahead of the curve in an increasingly dynamic and unpredictable market. However, it's important to strike a balance between speed and sustainability, ensuring that the company can maintain its momentum without burning out or sacrificing long-term stability.

All this change sees the role of the technology leader as changing from being the owner of "everything IT" to being a facilitator and a driver of digital transformation. Their executive peers must become (co-)owners of the technology. There is a fundamental fusion of business and tech. A fusion that, together with modern development tooling and cloud computing, is supporting the creation of a more flexible internal organization structure or ecosystem.

Does all that agility change Dr Mel Conway's law? Nope. It just gives you a whole new set of challenges at a whole new level. But the new level offers a much closer alignment between our organization structures and our IT solutions.

# CHAPTER 2

# The Core Concepts of AI

## Mastering the Essentials

*The true sign of intelligence is not knowledge but imagination.*
*~ Albert Einstein*

*AI will probably most likely lead to the end of the world,*
*but in the meantime, there'll be great companies.*
*~ Sam Altman*

*Any sufficiently advanced technology is indistinguishable from magic.*
*~ Arthur C. Clarke*

# Dive in at the Deep End

The term "artificial intelligence" was first coined by John McCarthy et al in a research proposal for a Dartmouth College conference in 1956.[9] "It may be speculated that a large part of human thought consists of manipulating words according to rules of reasoning and rules of conjecture," the paper posited.

Sixty-five years later, they were proved very right indeed.

While most organizations appreciate the potential of AI and feel a sense of urgency to get involved, a lack of confidence and vocabulary can form an obstacle to making meaningful progress. So let's dive in at the deep end.

The astounding public adoption rate of large language models (such as ChatGPT by OpenAI and Claude by Anthropic) evidences the enthusiasm with which people can adopt the tooling. However, in a workplace setting, organizations need to develop strategies to support and facilitate AI adoption through training and support. They need to integrate AI into the broader (agile) enterprise context, establish AI governance to guide ethical behaviour and manage risk, and align AI initiatives with organizational goals and values.

This chapter aims to clarify the fundamentals of AI, including key vocabulary and concepts. We'll also explore how AI systems learn through machine learning and discuss how AI can add business value. Getting value from AI investment is important, and we'll explore it further in the Continuous Product Innovation chapter.

AI is not magic; it is clever algorithms combined with a jaw-dropping quantity of data storage and computational power.

# A Little Bit of Science

The recent AI revolution, especially the surge in capabilities seen in large language models (LLMs), wasn't primarily due to groundbreaking new algorithms. Many of the algorithms that power modern AI, such as neural networks, have been around for decades. The real catalyst for change has been the exponential increase in compute power, together with the availability of what are called "large datasets" (large being a considerable understatement). Compute power was delivered primarily by repurposing the graphics processor units made by NVIDIA, originally to power games on PCs. The large dataset is, fundamentally, the World Wide Web (including Wikipedia, websites, blogs, academic papers and news channels) plus some book collections and a few other sources.

This combination has allowed existing algorithms to be applied on a scale and at a speed previously impossible, unlocking new possibilities in machine learning and AI applications. This computational leap forward has propelled AI from academic labs into real-world applications, driving innovations in fields ranging from healthcare to finance, and sparking a new era of innovation and excitement around AI's potential.

It's tempting to liken artificial intelligence to human intelligence. Although inspired by the workings of the human brain, the term AI is an unfortunate misnomer – a better term might be "machine intelligence". While there are similarities, AI and human brains work in fundamentally different ways.

In the human brain, a neuron fires based on the stimulus it receives from its inputs. If the stimulus is strong enough, the neuron activates and sends a signal to other neurons. This process is binary – it either happens or it doesn't. A neuron exerts influence by varying the frequency of the firing signals sent through neural pathways. Rapid firing is a strong signal; slower firing is a weaker signal. This biological mechanism enables thoughts, memories, muscle movement, and responses to our environment. It allows us to function as human beings.

An artificial neuron (a "node") in an artificial neural network (ANN) works by processing inputs with assigned weights, similar to the strength of synapse connections in the brain. Weights are crucial as they can adjust over time through learning, thereby improving the ANN's ability to make accurate predictions or decisions based on its inputs. It then adds these up and uses a function to decide its output. This output isn't a simple on or off but varies in value, reflecting the strength of the response. This method allows ANNs to simulate a simplified version of neural activity in the brain.

At its core, AI encompasses systems or machines that display human-like intelligence in tasks such as learning, reasoning, and problem-solving. However, it's important to differentiate between artificial general intelligence (AGI) and artificial narrow intelligence (ANI). AGI refers to machines with the ability to understand, learn, and apply knowledge across a broad range of tasks, mirroring human cognitive abilities. In contrast, today's AI technologies are predominantly ANI, designed to perform specific tasks – whether recognizing speech, translating languages, or diagnosing diseases – with proficiency often exceeding human capability in those narrow domains.

# How Does AI "Know"?

The essence of modern AI's learning capability is machine learning (ML), a subset of AI where algorithms learn through exposure to data, identifying patterns and taking decisions with minimal, or no, human direction. Tesla cars were not taught what a bicycle was, or a pedestrian or a traffic light; they learned by watching, akin to how an autodidactic person learns independently from various sources. Teslas learn through viewing (films of) the driving environment whereas LLMs learn by consuming voluminous quantities of text. Both are routes to AGI and will no doubt converge over time.

The process by which LLMs learn is core to their ability to understand and generate human-like text. At the heart of this capability is the concept of "training", where models are exposed to vast amounts of data, learning to recognize patterns, understand language nuances, and generate coherent, contextually relevant text. In short, you throw (almost) the whole internet at it, add in a collection of books, and see what happens.

Training an LLM involves feeding it a large corpus of text data. This could be anything from books, articles, and websites to more specialized datasets tailored to specific languages or domains. The model learns by adjusting the relationships between words and phrases to predict the next word in a sequence based on the words that come before it. And it does that by adjusting the weights in the nodes.

As the model processes more data, it refines its predictions, becoming increasingly sophisticated in its language understanding.

However, the efficiency of LLMs and their learning process isn't just about the algorithms and data; they also require vast computational resources… and a lot of electric power.

# Learning Models

There are three primary learning models – supervised learning, unsupervised learning, and reinforcement learning. Each play distinct roles in the AI landscape, influencing the capabilities of AI systems in various ways.

**Supervised learning** is the most commonly used model in AI applications today. In this approach, the AI system is trained on a labelled dataset, meaning that each example in the training set is paired with an answer key (the label). The goal is for the AI to learn the mapping between inputs and outputs, to predict the label from the inputs.

Supervised learning is like teaching a child with flashcards. You show the AI system lots of examples with the right answers until it gets really good at predicting outcomes. In a supervised learning task for image recognition, the AI might be trained with thousands of pictures, each labelled with the name of the object in the picture (like "cat", "dog", etc.). The AI uses this data to learn how to recognize and label new images correctly. This model is widely used in applications ranging from spam detection in emails to diagnosing medical images.

**Unsupervised learning**, in contrast, involves training an AI on data that has not been labelled. The AI tries to identify patterns and structures in the data without any explicit instructions on what it's looking for. This form of learning is particularly useful for exploratory data analysis, clustering, and association tasks where the relationships or groupings within the data are not known in advance.

Unsupervised learning is like letting an AI system explore a new city without a map. Instead of giving it labelled data, you just provide raw data and let it find patterns on its own. For example, imagine a retailer wants to understand customer purchasing behaviour. By feeding transaction data into an unsupervised learning model, the AI can uncover associations, like customers who buy product X often buy product Y two weeks later. This insight can drive strategic product placements and promotions. Another example is anomaly detection. In cybersecurity, an unsupervised model can analyse network traffic and identify unusual patterns that might indicate a cyber threat, even if no previous examples of such threats exist – more on this later.

**Reinforcement learning** is a model inspired by behavioural psychology, where an AI learns to make a sequence of decisions by interacting with a dynamic environment. The AI receives rewards or penalties in response to its actions, guiding it to learn the best strategies over time. This model is often used in scenarios requiring a balance of immediate and future actions, such as robotic navigation and online game playing. A popular example is AI systems developed to play and master complex games like Go or chess, where the system learns winning strategies by playing numerous games against itself and incrementally improving through trial and error.

Each of these models offers a different approach to learning and decision-making, providing AI researchers and developers with powerful tools to solve a wide range of problems. By integrating these models, AI systems can achieve higher levels of understanding and functionality, adapting their behaviours to optimize performance across various tasks and environments.

## AI, LLMs and Robots

The fusion of robotics and AI is revolutionizing how machines interact with the world, creating intelligent systems capable of performing complex tasks with minimal human intervention. Robotics provides the physical framework, comprising sensors, actuators, and mechanical components, while AI powers these systems with the ability to perceive, reason, and adapt.

For example, the Boston Dynamics' robot, Spot,[10] is an agile quadruped robot used in various industries, from construction to healthcare. Spot uses AI to navigate challenging environments, avoid obstacles, and perform tasks like inspecting hazardous areas.

LLMs are now being used to train robots to be more sensitive towards human beings and to navigate the world more accurately through reinforcement learning. In other words, the LLM acts as a coach for the robot. This approach also allows robots to be trained wholly in a virtual, computer environment, before being let loose in the real world – a useful damage-control exercise.

As these technologies advance, challenges such as ethical considerations, real-world complexity, and maintaining a balance between autonomy and human control become increasingly critical. These developments not only push the boundaries of what's possible but also redefine the roles robots will play in our daily lives and industries, heralding a future where intelligent machines are integral to our world.

Elon Musk has predicted that the market for (humanoid) robots will be worth trillions. (I'll have one for the laundry and the washing-up please.)

# Humans in AI Learning

Can you trust 100% of what an AI/LLM model tells you? Well, no. Or at least, not yet. AIs must be trustworthy, reliable, unbiased, and capable of being impartial. In these early days of LLMs, they're clever, but far from perfect.

Thousands of hours of human effort are involved in training AI models. The young AI training industry is already worth billions in annual revenue. The collaboration between human understanding and machine learning is a dynamic process, aiming to ensure that AI models not only function efficiently but also align with our ethical and societal values. (This raises some interesting questions about ethical and societal values as most LLMs are trained on a mix of Western values and English language data – but that's a debate beyond the scope of these pages.)

## Data Labelling

At the heart of human AI training lies the meticulous process of data annotation and labelling: this is a cat and this is a dog; this is a quark; this is a picture of a potentially cancerous cell; these words represent a positive emotion and these a negative. Imagine vast amounts of raw data, unstructured and chaotic, akin to an enormous library where books lack titles and genres.

Humans step in to organize this data, tagging and annotating it with context and meaning. This task is often handled by dedicated annotators, transforming the data into a structured format that AI systems can learn from. The sheer scale of this endeavour is immense, with companies employing thousands of individuals to sift through and label data, ensuring that AI systems are fed with accurate and relevant information.

## Reinforcement Learning from Human Feedback

Beyond data annotation, human feedback plays a key role in refining AI behaviour through techniques like Reinforcement Learning From Human Feedback (RLHF). Here, humans evaluate the AI's performance, providing scores and rankings for its outputs. This feedback loop guides the AI in understanding human preferences and ethical considerations. For instance, when training a language model, human reviewers assess the coherence, relevance, and appropriateness of the generated text.

Human oversight extends to bias mitigation and ethical governance. Bias in AI can stem from unrepresentative training data or algorithmic shortcomings. Humans meticulously review AI outputs, aiming to identify and address these biases.

## Human-in-the-Loop

The relationship between humans and AI is not static; it is an evolving partnership. Human-in-the-loop systems exemplify this dynamic interaction, where humans continuously monitor and refine AI performance. In fields like autonomous driving, human drivers provide valuable data that improves the AI's decision-making capabilities.

Similarly, in content moderation, human reviewers work alongside AI to scrutinize and manage online content, ensuring compliance with community standards and removing harmful material. There's a lot of work to be done here, and the big social media platforms are often criticized for not putting sufficient investment into preventing and taking down deepfakes and harmful content.

### Walmart's AI-Powered Store

Walmart's Intelligent Retail Lab (IRL) is an AI-powered store that focuses on enhancing the customer experience and operational efficiency. IRL is a fully operational store, utilizing AI to monitor inventory levels in real time. Cameras and sensors track products on shelves, ensuring they are always stocked and providing data to streamline store management.
This technology enables Walmart to optimize operations, improve inventory accuracy, and better meet customer demands.

# What Is a GPT?

GPT stands for generative pre-trained transformer – the model that took the world by storm when released to the public by OpenAI. Each component of the acronym reveals something important about how the model works and its place in the AI landscape. This approach is widely used in the field of AI.

## Generative

This indicates that GPT is designed to generate text. It can produce coherent, contextually relevant sentences and paragraphs that often resemble human-written text. This capability makes it useful for a wide range of applications, from writing assistance and content creation to dialogue systems and more.

## Pre-trained

Before a GPT can do anything useful, it undergoes an extensive pre-training phase (see above).

## Transformer

The architecture underlying GPT is called a transformer, a type of neural network designed specifically for handling sequences of data, such as sentences in natural language. The transformer architecture is notable for its use of the so-called attention mechanism, which allows the model to weigh the importance of different words within an input sequence when generating each word in an output sequence. So, for example, if we say "sitting on the doormat, the dog ate its food", the model will "understand" that the word "its" refers to the dog and not the doormat.

The transformer architecture originated in Google's labs in 2017 (making it rather sour for them that OpenAI beat them to market) and was published in a paper, *Attention Is All You Need.*[12] The concept of attention is central to the transformer architecture and, by extension, to GPT. It enables the model to manage long-range dependencies in text, meaning it can "remember" and utilize information from earlier parts of the text while working on later parts. This ability is crucial for understanding complex sentences, maintaining coherence over long passages, and generating text that is relevant to the given context.

# AI and Multimedia

## Images

There are two parts to AI image processing: image recognition and image generation. Image recognition and generation systems employ sophisticated neural network architectures to interpret and create visual content. These systems are trained on extensive datasets (such as ImageNet[13]) containing images labelled with their corresponding descriptions or categories. Through this training, they learn to identify patterns, shapes, and colours that define different objects and scenes. After a model has seen, say, ten thousand pictures of a cat, it knows what a cat looks like to an extremely high degree of accuracy.

For image recognition, such as distinguishing a cat from a dog, the system analyses the input image by breaking it down into smaller, manageable features – pixels, groups of pixels and groups of groups of pixels: a bit like zooming in on Google Earth to reveal increasing levels of granularity. By comparing these features against known patterns (of cats and dogs) it has learned during training, the system can classify the image as depicting a cat or a dog based on distinguishing characteristics in its dataset.

For image generation, systems apply a different approach. They understand context and visual elements from textual descriptions, synthesizing this information to produce images that match given criteria. Whether generating a picture of a cat, a dog, or an entirely new creature, these models draw on their learned repository of features to create coherent and often surprisingly realistic images. Like a cat and a dog on the moon at sunset.

## Video

In the area of video, AI technologies are being used to automate editing, enhance image quality, and enable sophisticated effects that were once the sole domain of high-end production studios. For instance, AI-driven algorithms can now analyse hours of raw footage to identify the most engaging scenes, suggest edits, or even create highlight reels without human intervention. This not only speeds up the production process but also reduces costs and makes high-quality video production accessible to a broader range of creators.

## Audio

In audio, AI is making equally significant strides. Sophisticated algorithms are used for everything from improving sound quality to generating entirely new compositions. AI systems can remove background noise, balance sound levels, and enhance clarity, which is particularly beneficial in podcast production and music mastering. AI is also being explored in the creation of music, where it analyses vast datasets of music to learn styles and compositions, subsequently creating new music pieces that can serve as inspiration or ready-to-use tracks for artists. This capability is not just changing how music is produced but is also pushing the boundaries of creativity, offering new tools that artists and producers can use to express their ideas.

# Inference – The Execution Phase in AI

While learning and training are often regarded as the input phase for AI, the process of executing queries, responding to new data and creating outputs is known as "inference".

Inference in AI refers to the process of applying pre-trained models to draw conclusions, predict outcomes, classify information, or generate insights. It represents the execution phase where the model uses its acquired knowledge to make decisions or predictions based on new input data.

For example, in a neural network trained to recognize images of cats and dogs, inference is the process where the model analyses a new image and determines whether it depicts a cat or a dog. This relies on the weights and biases the model learned during the training phase to interpret and categorize new data accurately.

In the context of natural language processing (NLP), inference plays a crucial role in enabling AI systems to understand and generate human language. When interacting with an LLM, such as ChatGPT, inference powers the entire process. Broadly speaking, there are three key components to this:

- **Input processing:** The model receives and processes your text input, typically breaking it down into tokens (small units of meaning) and normalizing the text to prepare it for analysis.

- **Model application:** The pre-trained language model processes these tokens through its layers, using its learned knowledge to generate a coherent and contextually relevant response. This step involves complex mechanisms like attention layers, which allow the model to focus on the most relevant parts of the input.
- **Output generation:** The system produces the response you see, decoding the model's predictions into human-readable text. This output draws on patterns, context, and knowledge encoded within the model.

At a fundamental level (albeit ludicrously oversimplified), inference in NLP can be thought of as a sophisticated next-word prediction algorithm. It predicts the next word in a sentence based on the context provided by preceding words, the nature of the query, and common patterns in human language.

But inference goes far beyond simple next-word prediction:

**Language Translation:** Inference enables the model to translate entire texts from one language to another by understanding not just individual words, but the grammar, syntax, and cultural nuances embedded in language.

**Text Summarizing:** The model can condense long documents into concise summaries, identifying key points and relevant details without losing the original intent or meaning. This can be useful, for example, in summarising a scientific paper or a long email chain.

**Question Answering:** Advanced models can read and comprehend text passages to answer specific questions, even when the answer requires synthesizing information from different parts of the text. This capability relies on the model's understanding of context, relevance, and the relationships between concepts – even the concept of a "concept".

**Creative Content Generation:** Inference also powers the generation of creative content, such as writing poetry, composing music, or crafting fictional narratives. The model uses its vast training data to produce content that is not only contextually appropriate but also appears to be creative and original.

**Complex Decision-Making:** Beyond language tasks, inference enables AI systems to perform complex decision-making, such as recommending products, optimizing logistics, or even assisting in medical diagnosis. These tasks require the model to analyse vast amounts of data, recognize patterns, and make informed decisions that align with specific goals or constraints.

These advanced capabilities illustrate the incredible power of inference. Inference is about leveraging a deep understanding of data, context and relationships to perform sophisticated tasks that can rival, and in some cases surpass, human abilities.

## Real-Time Inference

In many applications, AI systems must make predictions or decisions instantly; a capability known as "real-time inference". For example, autonomous vehicles rely on real-time inference to process sensory data and make split-second decisions that ensure safe navigation. Similarly, real-time language translation must instantly convert spoken words into another language, requiring the AI to process and generate outputs almost instantaneously.

### AI in Healthcare

AI has the potential to transform healthcare globally by addressing numerous challenges: from improving access to care in underserved regions like Africa to enhancing diagnostic precision and personalized treatments in the West.

NHS England[14] is spearheading digital transformation in healthcare by integrating electronic health records (EHRs), telehealth services, and AI-driven diagnostic tools. This initiative aims to enhance patient care by improving efficiency and accessibility.

AI tools are utilized for predicting patient admission rates, managing bed occupancy, and diagnosing conditions from medical scans, leading to better resource management and quicker patient diagnoses.

This transformation isn't just about technology; it's also about transforming the way healthcare is delivered.

## Edge Inference

Inference isn't confined to large data centres or cloud environments; it is increasingly performed at the "edge", meaning on devices like smartphones, home appliances, or in embedded systems within machinery. Edge inference allows AI models to operate locally, reducing latency, enhancing privacy, and enabling functionality in environments with limited or no internet connectivity. A smartphone's camera app might use edge inference to apply real-time filters or enhancements without sending data to the cloud. This capability is particularly valuable in applications where speed, privacy, and operational independence are crucial.

### AI in the Office

Google and Microsoft are adding AI features into their office products. Together, these two players dominate the office automation market.
Both are claiming considerable productivity gains from their new AI capabilities. An Avanade (part-owned by Microsoft) large-scale survey[15] reports that over 90% of organizations believe they need to adopt an AI-first operating model to stay competitive, yet many lack the necessary skills and AI frameworks to support this transition. There is a critical need for upskilling and robust governance policies to manage AI risks and align initiatives with corporate values.
According to Avanade, employees estimate that Microsoft Copilot will impact up to twenty hours of their work week, primarily by automating repetitive tasks and inspiring creative ideas. Even if vastly overestimated, this potentially translates into very considerable cost savings.

# Applications on Top of AI Models

The amazing value of LLMs has already been discovered by millions. But what does the future hold in terms of applying this technology to real-world problems?

CEO of OpenAI Sam Altman says (in an interview with Reid Hoffman[16]) that a lot of value will be created in a new "middle layer" on top of GPT. We're already seeing a growing ecosystem of applications built on the ChatGPT foundation – some of these will be bandwagon-jumpers; others may be great value creators.

What might the new middle layer comprise? In short, almost anything a human can do: computer programming, medical diagnosis, biotech, financial advice, share price guidance, customer service chatbots (that actually work), and answering exam questions.

# AI versus Human Thinking

## Left-Brain versus Right-Brain Thinking

The human brain has two halves, or hemispheres, which are connected by the tissue of the corpus callosum. These two halves are physically separate, apart from the few hundred million-odd fibres that connect them. Neuroscientists have found that the left hemisphere tends to deal with logic, mathematics, language, and specifics, while the right hemisphere deals more with abstraction, spatial awareness, creativity, art and music.

In *The Master and His Emissary*,[17] Iain McGilchrist explores the profound differences between the left and right hemispheres of the brain and their impact on Western culture. The left hemisphere is depicted as analytical, detail-oriented, and focused on narrow, precise tasks. It excels in language, logic, and sequential thinking but tends to miss the bigger picture. In contrast, the right hemisphere is holistic, intuitive, and capable of understanding context and nuance. It is adept at recognizing patterns, emotions, and broader, more interconnected aspects of reality.

McGilchrist argues that modern Western society has become overly dominated by the left hemisphere's reductive and mechanistic view, sidelining the more integrative and empathetic perspective of the right hemisphere, leading to cultural imbalances and societal challenges.

An overreliance on AI for our decision-making may exacerbate the problem of too much left-hemisphere thinking. Yet it may also allow us a deeper understanding of what it is to be human, as opposed to biological intelligence systems. We may also like to revisit the very definition of intelligence – but these discussions go a little beyond our scope here.

Human beings can take time to think about a problem from various angles, to postulate, hypothesize, cogitate, and contemplate an issue. If we don't need to take a decision immediately, we can allow our right brain the freedom to approach the problem creatively, holistically, and spiritually, applying our values, morals, and ethics to provide a sense of direction. This process is bound to be, to some extent, subconscious (with echoes of the AI explainability conundrum discussed below).

LLMs can make it appear as if they are doing right-brained thinking, but they're not. They are more comparable to left-brain thinking – goal seeking and result driven. I'm not discounting that, at some point in time, AI systems may "understand" paths to responses that are not exclusively or entirely rational, but it might take a while.

AI's ability to truly replicate the holistic, intuitive, and emotionally nuanced processing of the right hemisphere remains limited. When we walk into a room or onto a stage, we can feel an energy; we can look at a sunset, the night sky, or a magnificent mountain range with a sense of awe; look at our children or grandchildren with pure joy; look at our partner and feel love and connection. Explaining these emotions in language is simply not possible, so we turn to music, poetry, images and rituals to "describe" what we feel… and they impact on our decisions. AI struggles with tasks that require an understanding beyond pattern recognition, such as exhibiting true creativity or understanding nuanced human emotions, which are often influenced by a myriad of factors beyond the observable data.

We'll return to this fundamental discussion in the Leadership and People chapter.

## Transfer Learning

Humans are also particularly adept at transfer learning, which involves applying knowledge gained in one context to new, often unrelated, situations. This capability allows for high levels of creativity, as it enables the synthesis of seemingly unrelated concepts into novel ideas and solutions. This cognitive flexibility is not strictly dependent on direct experience or explicit similarity between tasks. For example, the problem-solving skills developed in one scientific discipline, like physics, can unexpectedly provide insights into an unrelated field like economics. This ability is crucial for innovation and creative thinking because it allows individuals to draw abstract parallels and amalgamate information across domains.

This innate capability significantly enhances human creativity. By connecting disparate ideas, humans can create innovative solutions and concepts that might seem unrelated at first glance. This synthesis can lead to breakthroughs in art, science, and technology. For instance, the concept of biomimicry in design is based on this ability to apply patterns and solutions from nature to solve human engineering and design challenges. The development of Velcro, inspired by the way burrs stick to animal fur, is a classic example of this kind of creative problem-solving. Transfer learning not only enriches our understanding and ability to navigate multiple spheres but also underscores the uniquely human capacity to innovate and think creatively.

## The Black Box Dilemma

The black-box nature of many AI systems complicates explainability, making it difficult to understand how they arrive at some results. In other words, we cannot know how an AI system arrived at any particular outcome. In that sense, they are similar to our own brains: we understand the brain at a micro level (neuron) and a macro level (architecture) but cannot trace each thought that arrives on our consciousness back to its origins.

In fields where certain decisions may have significant consequences (military, law, health etc.), we may like to get a very clear answer as to how the AI arrived at a particular conclusion. In theory, it's conceivable that we could investigate and explain how an AI system arrived at a specific conclusion. However, in practice, the models are so colossal and complex that deciphering the process becomes unfeasible.

## Bias

The effectiveness of AI often hinges on the availability of large, well-annotated datasets, which are not always available. Bias in AI, stemming from biased data or algorithms, remains a significant issue, affecting fairness and accuracy. Addressing these challenges is critical for the responsible development and deployment of AI technologies.

## Societal Impact

This book takes a positive view of AI, but a note of caution may be appropriate. For those individuals who can rise to the challenges and equip themselves with the skills and flexibility to master the technologies, the future will be rosy.

However, there may also be a significant percentage of the population who may not be able to participate fully in the new order. Thomas Piketty, author of the surprising economics bestseller, *Capital in the Twenty-First Century*[18] (written before the AI boom), argues the case that current projected levels of economic growth will lead to a situation whereby the inequalities between the wealthy and the rest will no longer be compatible with our values of democracy and meritocracy. He alerts us to the disappearing wealth of the middle classes and the potential impact on society as a whole. Our society will have to change to ensure all people can participate and share in the wealth that AI can bring. It's up to us.

# Crafting an AI Strategy

This book is fundamentally about building a solid AI and digital strategy, and in the chapters that follow, we'll dive deeper into the elements of this. But for now, I'd like to focus on the core aspects of AI strategy – those specific considerations that set it apart from the more usual aspects of crafting a business or technology strategy.

Crafting a successful AI strategy must involve a wide range of disciplines and stakeholders from across the organization to address the unique properties of AI. Integrating AI into an organization's strategy isn't just about adopting new technology – it's about rethinking how the business operates and empowers its people. In what Charles Handy eloquently dubbed *The Age of Unreason*[19], the most successful organizations will be those best capable of managing change.

**Business alignment:** Arguably obvious, but it's crucial to align your AI initiatives with your business objectives: identify a few key areas where AI can have the most impact, whether that's reducing costs, enhancing customer experience, or driving new revenue streams. Prioritize these high-impact areas to achieve early successes that demonstrate value (financial or otherwise) and drive broader adoption and enthusiasm across the organization.

**Scalability:** Consider how easily the early projects can be scaled and integrated into everyday operations. Some initiatives might deliver quick wins, while others will take longer to mature, but the aim is to build a solid foundation for scaling AI and upskilling the organization over time.

**Focus on the human element:** While AI is driven by algorithms, the success of your AI strategy hinges on the right talent. It's important to attract and develop the skills needed to power your AI initiatives, whether that involves hiring new experts or upskilling your existing team. Cultivating a culture of continuous learning will be essential to keep pace with the rapid evolution of AI (as we shall see in the Leadership and People chapter).

**Data quality:** is a critical component. The effectiveness of your AI efforts depends on the quality of your data. This means establishing strong data management practices that ensure your data is clean, reliable, and well-governed. Data isn't a technology issue; it's a strategic asset that requires attention across the entire organization.

**Consider the ethical implications:** As AI becomes more integrated into decision-making, it's important to have clear guidelines in place to address issues such as bias, transparency, and accountability. Developing a governance framework that ensures your AI initiatives are ethical and fair will help build trust and ensure the long-term success of your AI strategy.

# CHAPTER SUMMARY

AI is not magic but a combination of clever algorithms, vast data storage, and immense computational power, with machine learning being the essence of modern AI's learning capability.

While AI has the potential to revolutionize various industries and solve complex problems, it also has limitations and societal implications that need to be addressed through responsible development and deployment.

## Get Value from AI – Short-term and Long-term

**Align AI with business objectives:** craft an AI strategy that aligns with business objectives and includes the particular factors that AI success requires. Let me strengthen that a little: review your business objectives, indeed your entire operating model, in the light of AI.

**Experiment and innovate:** identify two or three high-impact use cases for AI and get started. Focus on pilots that can move the needle, like automating customer service, office productivity or enhancing financial reporting. Consider the AI-specific business risks and opportunities the projects present, and how easily they can be scaled and integrated into everyday operations.

**Foster collaboration:** encourage collaboration between business domain experts and AI professionals to develop innovative solutions that tackle real-world challenges and deliver organizational value.

**Implement ethical governance:** establish governance frameworks and ethical guidelines to ensure AI is used transparently, accountably, and without bias. Engage in policy debates to shape responsible AI development.

**Release budget for resources:** allocate sufficient budget for cloud and AI computational resources and datasets. Good AI is not cheap.

# CHAPTER 3

# Cloud

# Computing

## Increase Agility, Speed and Scalability, and Reduce Cost

*To change something, build a new model that makes the existing model obsolete.*
*~ Buckminster Fuller*

*Every kid coming out of Harvard, every kid coming out of school now thinks he can be the next Mark Zuckerberg, and with these new technologies like cloud computing, he actually has a shot.*
*~ Marc Andreessen*

*The cloud services companies of all sizes; the cloud is for everyone.*
*The cloud is a democracy.*
*~ Marc Benioff*

# Cloud is a Fundamental Shift

Cloud computing represents a fundamental shift in how businesses acquire, use, and manage IT resources. The cloud model allows companies to access computing infrastructure over the internet, offering significant flexibility and scalability. This infrastructure includes all the foundational hardware, software, networks, and data centres that support the processing, storage, and transmission of data.

The cloud is housed in a global network of massive data centres connected by high-bandwidth optical cables. Each cloud service provider (CSP) has its own collection of data centres that are strategically placed to provide maximum physical security, high-bandwidth internet access and a sustainable electricity supply at lowest cost. So-called "hyperscale" data centres are the size of a dozen or so football fields and consume the electricity equivalent of powering up to a hundred thousand homes.

On top of this massive global real-estate portfolio and computer hardware infrastructure, sophisticated software forms the bedrock of this modern digital infrastructure. The basic cloud services provide for the provisioning of virtual implementations of traditional computer resources: a client may ask for processing capacity, or a firewall, or memory, or storage, but what they actually get may be a small piece of a much larger shared resource.

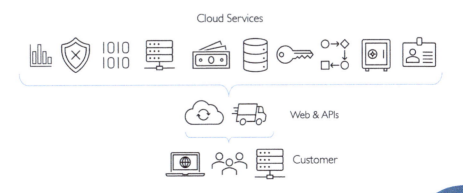

Cloud Services

Web & APIs

Customer

However, cloud software goes far beyond basic provisioning of resources to the orchestration of advanced services. CSPs offer hundreds of services, including overall governance, compliance, advanced security, cost management, application management services, DevOps support, sophisticated billing, machine learning, analytics, and much more.

Cloud computing is fundamental in driving digital transformation, providing the infrastructure necessary to deploy advanced technologies like artificial intelligence and big data analytics swiftly and at scale. This capability allows businesses to experiment and innovate more freely, without the constraints imposed by physical hardware limitations such as lead times to deployment, capital expenditure, and ongoing updates and maintenance.

# Cloud Service Models

Cloud services are broadly categorized into three models, each serving distinct needs and providing different levels of management and customization: infrastructure as a service, platform as a service and application software as a service — inelegantly abbreviated to IaaS, PaaS and SaaS.

## Infrastructure as a Service

IaaS is the most basic cloud service model, offering compute power, network, and storage capabilities as on-demand services from the cloud providers. IaaS is comparable to running your own data centre, but on someone else's premises.

## Platform as a Service

PaaS provides a higher level of abstraction compared to IaaS, offering everything from network and storage to development tools, database management systems, and business analytics tools, all integrated into a single platform. This setup allows developers to focus on the creation of software without worrying about operating systems, software updates, storage, or infrastructure. PaaS solutions are a powerful accelerator for software developers to build applications quicker without dealing with underlying infrastructure.

## Software as a Service

SaaS stretches the definition of cloud to business applications. Whereas IaaS and PaaS are aimed mostly at the tech engineering community, SaaS is aimed at business users. SaaS delivers software applications over the internet, on a subscription basis, managed by third-party vendors. Applications like Gmail, Salesforce, SAP, Oracle, Zendesk, ServiceNow and Microsoft 365 are examples of SaaS.

# Deployment Models

Cloud computing will be integral to IT strategies across all industries. The transition to cloud-based systems isn't just a matter of choice but a necessity to remain competitive and agile. However, the shift to the cloud isn't one-size-fits-all, particularly for sectors where data privacy, security, and regulatory compliance are paramount.

Many are apparently struggling with cloud adoption: according to the 2023 State of Cloud report[20], 51% of technology leaders are investing in cloud, yet only 27% report that their cloud initiatives are driving increased customer value.

Firms are mistaking the adoption of cloud technology for true digital transformation without actually implementing the transformative practices that the cloud enables.

Some larger organizations, such as government institutions, security agencies, global banks or healthcare providers, who are concerned about privacy to the point of paranoia, are hesitant to migrate to a public cloud… and perhaps rightly so. However, there are options available for these industries, as we shall explore below. Choosing the right cloud strategy model is driven by business needs, data sensitivity, and required levels of control over the environment:

## Public Cloud

Public clouds are owned and operated by third-party cloud service providers, delivering their computing resources over the internet. AWS, Microsoft Azure, and Google Cloud are examples of public clouds.

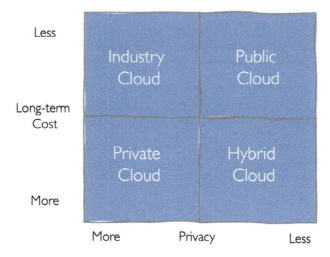

The fact that public cloud offers "less" privacy is relative – it is still a highly robust infrastructure offering sufficient privacy options for most workloads.

Public cloud will be the choice for most organizations as it provides the richness of full cloud facilities and good security at a reasonable cost.

## Private Cloud

A private cloud refers to resources used exclusively by one business or organization. A private cloud can be physically located on a company's on-premises data centre, or it could be hosted by a third-party service provider. This arrangement offers potentially more control and security, making it suitable for enterprises that need to meet strict data security and compliance requirements.

## Hybrid Cloud

This model combines public and private clouds (or on-premises data centres), allowing data and applications to move between the two environments. This is the halfway house and will, for many, be the most logical way to adopt cloud. Legacy applications, or applications with very high privacy or security requirements, can be retained on-premises in organization-owned data centres, while new and innovative applications can be developed in a cloud environment.

## Industry-Specific Cloud

The growing demand for industry-specific cloud solutions and specialized data centres stems from the unique needs, regulations, and challenges faced by different sectors. These tailored offerings allow organizations to reap the benefits of cloud computing while ensuring appropriate levels of compliance.

For instance, healthcare clouds emphasize data security and compliance with regulations. Financial clouds will create secure and compliant environments for hosting financial applications.

### Sovereign (AI) Cloud

Sovereign cloud is a special case of industry cloud. It refers to a cloud computing environment where data is stored and processed entirely within the jurisdiction of a specific country, complying with that nation's regulations on data privacy, security, and sovereignty. This concept is now expanding into sovereign AI, where nations not only store their data locally but also build AI factories to act on that data.

This shift reflects a growing recognition that data is a national asset, akin to land, sea, and air, and must be protected accordingly. At the time of writing, a number of countries are building sovereign state AI (cloud) factories, including: Japan, US, UK, India, Canada, France, Italy, Singapore and Malaysia.[21]

### Multi-Cloud

By employing multiple cloud providers, organizations can ensure that their operations are not overly dependent on a single vendor, thus avoiding the risks associated with vendor lock-in.

However, the adoption of a multi-cloud strategy introduces complexities that necessitate careful management and integration tools. Organizations must manage disparate cloud environments, each with its own set of tools, APIs, and management interfaces.

# Scalability and Elasticity

Two critical features that are driving the success of cloud are scalability and elasticity. These concepts are often conflated, but they serve distinct roles in managing IT resources and have different financial impacts.

Scalability refers to a system's capacity to accommodate longer-term growth. In cloud computing, scalability can be achieved either vertically or horizontally. Vertical scalability involves adding more power to an existing machine, such as increasing CPU or RAM, whereas horizontal scalability means adding more machines to a system, such as adding additional servers.

Elasticity, on the other hand, is the ability of a system to automatically adjust the resources it uses in response to shorter-term changing demand. This flexibility ensures that resources are allocated in the most efficient manner possible, growing when demand increases and shrinking when demand decreases.

In practice, managing scalability and elasticity involves sophisticated orchestration and automation tools. Cloud providers offer services that automatically adjust resource allocation based on predefined policies.

The financial implications of scalability and elasticity are significant. Traditionally, businesses had to predict their maximum load and provision enough hardware to handle it, leading to substantial upfront costs and often resulting in underutilized resources. Cloud computing's pay-as-you-go model changes this dynamic by charging users only for the resources they actually use. This model is particularly advantageous for businesses with variable workloads, such as e-commerce sites that experience traffic spikes due to promotional offers or certain times of the day.

Cost savings from effective management of scalability and elasticity can be substantial. The reduction in hardware investments, maintenance costs, and energy consumption contributes to lower operational costs.

The scalability provided by cloud allows businesses to innovate and experiment without substantial financial risk. Start-ups, for instance, can launch new services and scale them rapidly if they gain traction, without the need for significant upfront capital. However, it's essential to manage cloud resources carefully to maximize these financial benefits. Uncontrolled scaling can lead to runaway costs, as resources can be inadvertently overprovisioned.

# Disaster Recovery and Business Continuity

Disaster recovery (DR) and business continuity (BC) are important for keeping organizations running smoothly and bouncing back from disruptions. DR and BC are often trade-offs between cost and service level requirements. There is an inverse ratio between service availability and cost – and offering a global non-stop service is expensive.

Conceptually, DR and BC are not any different in a cloud setting to a private data centre environment: they need to be thought through and architected into the design of infrastructures and applications. Cloud service providers do make it a lot easier. They provide a multitude of services to allow you to configure the service level you require.

An important part of DR and BC cloud strategies is deciding where to store cloud data and run cloud apps. Choosing the right cloud "regions" (geographically separate data centre areas) is key. Cloud providers offer multiple regions worldwide, each designed to operate independently.

Using multiple regions to store data and run applications makes a system more resilient. If a disaster hits one region, you can quickly switch to another unaffected region, keeping downtime to a minimum. This geographical spread of resources also guards against local problems like natural disasters, power outages, or network issues.

# Security and Compliance Architecture

In a cloud environment, security compliance and architecture are fundamental to protecting data and business continuity. Organizations generally have to adhere to various regulatory requirements and industry standards, which necessitates robust security measures. This includes implementing identity and access management (IAM) systems, adopting zero-trust models, and ensuring data encryption and network security. We'll take a deeper dive into cybersecurity in a separate chapter, but these three are foundational for cloud and offer a sense of why cloud is not simply "someone else's computer".

## Identity and Access Management (IAM)

IAM is crucial for controlling who has access to what resources in a cloud environment. Cloud providers offer extensive IAM services that enable organizations to manage user permissions and enforce the principle of least privilege. By using IAM, businesses can ensure that only authorized users can access sensitive data and critical applications, reducing the risk of unauthorized access and data breaches.

## Zero-Trust Models

The zero-trust security model operates on the principle that no entity, whether inside or outside the network, should be trusted by default. In cloud, this involves continuously verifying the identity of users and devices before granting access to resources. Implementing a zero-trust architecture requires multi-factor authentication (MFA), micro-segmentation of networks, and continuous monitoring of user activity.

## Encryption and Network Security

Encryption plays a key role in protecting data both at rest (say, in a database) and in transit (across a network) within a cloud environment. Cloud providers offer built-in encryption services that automatically encrypt data stored in databases, file systems, and backups. Additionally, transport layer security (TLS) ensures that data transmitted over the network is encrypted, safeguarding it from interception and tampering.

Together, these security measures form a security architecture that helps organizations meet compliance requirements, protect sensitive data, and maintain a strong security posture in the cloud. It's like having a top-notch security team on duty 24/7, ensuring your cloud environment is not only compliant with all the necessary regulations but also ready to fend off digital threats.

# Cloud Adoption: Technology Strategies

If you're a start-up, you're probably "born" cloud native. (If not, why not?) However, if you have a non-cloud suite of applications running in a data centre, then you will need to consider migration. Migrating existing systems and infrastructure to the cloud requires careful planning and execution to ensure minimal disruption and maximum benefits. Several strategies can be employed, each suited to different needs and goals.

## Lift and Shift

This approach involves moving applications to the cloud with minimal changes. It's relatively quick and cost-effective, allowing organizations to benefit from the cloud's scalability and reliability without extensive modifications. However, it is unlikely to optimize cloud-native features and could lead to suboptimal performance and higher costs over time.

## Replatforming

Also known as "lift, tinker, and shift", this strategy involves making a few cloud optimizations without changing the core architecture of the applications. For example, replacing on-premises databases with managed cloud databases can improve performance and reduce management overhead. Replatforming strikes a balance between the simplicity of lift and shift and the extensive changes required for refactoring.

## Refactoring

This strategy involves rearchitecting applications to take full advantage of cloud-native features. It can significantly improve scalability, performance, and cost efficiency. Refactoring often includes adopting microservices, serverless architectures with cloud-native databases and storage solutions. While this approach offers the most long-term benefits, it requires substantial effort, time, and expertise.

**Spotify: From Data Centre to Full Cloud**[23]

Spotify selected Google Cloud Platform (GCP) for a full migration, avoiding the complexities of hybrid or multi-cloud setups. This extensive project involved over one hundred teams, two thousand services and one hundred petabytes of data. They employed a mix of "lift and shift" and full rewrites to ensure a seamless service transition.

Spotify successfully decommissioned all on-premises data centres after about two years, achieving significant improvements in scalability and operational efficiency.

This migration enabled Spotify to innovate faster, leverage advanced technologies like machine learning, and enhance their data processing capabilities. The transition also facilitated better resource management and cost efficiency, allowing engineers to focus more on product development and less on infrastructure maintenance.

# Cloud Adoption: Organizational Strategies

Migrating to the cloud significantly impacts an organization's human resources and operational dynamics, including IT, legal, compliance, and finance departments. This transition necessitates retraining and affects how the entire organization functions.

IT staff must develop new skills in cloud architecture, service management, and automation. Training programmes and certifications from cloud providers are essential. These new skills include managing virtual resources, using managed services, and implementing cloud security best practices.

Legal and compliance teams must navigate new challenges, such as auditing cloud providers, managing complex cloud contracts, and addressing data sovereignty issues. They need to ensure compliance with international regulations like GDPR, DORA and CCPA when data is stored in different jurisdictions. Additionally, they must implement new monitoring tools and conduct regular audits to verify that cloud services adhere to industry standards such as PCI DSS.

The financial model may change from outright purchasing, lease, and capital expenditure to pay-as-you-go (operational expenditure), impacting budgeting and cash flow. The cloud services' pay-as-you-go model provides flexibility but requires new cost management strategies. Finance teams must adapt to dynamic billing, optimize resource allocation, and monitor usage to avoid unexpected expenses.

Cloud migration is a change management process and effective communication and collaboration across departments are vital. Implementing a structured change management process, engaging leadership, and providing continuous support will help manage the transition smoothly.

### Capital One's Cloud Migration[24]

Capital One's switch to a cloud-first strategy with AWS was all about boosting efficiency and innovation. They moved away from traditional data centres to AWS's infrastructure, which allowed them to deploy applications faster, enhance security, and reduce costs. This move also improved their disaster recovery capabilities and enabled real-time data management, making them more agile in responding to customer needs. The transition wasn't merely technical – it involved a cultural shift. Capital One invested in training its tech team, promoting a culture of continuous learning and agile practices. This cloud-first approach enabled them to deliver personalized and secure customer experiences, integrating AI and data at scale.

# Is Cloud for Everyone?

Cloud offers many features and a promise for future growth. However, it may not be for everyone. If your software does high-frequency trading on a stock exchange where milliseconds count, then you might want to run on "bare metal" in a location that is as physically close (to reduce latency) to the exchanges as possible.

Equally, if you're running an extremely confidential database, say, an aggregate of all medical data in your country, or a military or intelligence application, then data protection and privacy may be more paramount than speed of deployment and easy access to AI.

Customers with stable software and steady workloads may also gain little advantage from going cloud as it may only serve to increase costs.

Cloud is not for everyone, but for most businesses, the pros will outweigh the cons.

# The Future of Cloud

It's already impossible for on-premises tech teams to keep up with cloud development, but we've really only just started and the developments will be ongoing at speed in the coming years.

## Serverless

One of the most prominent trends is the rise of "serverless" computing. This paradigm allows developers to build and run applications without worrying about the underlying infrastructure, automatically scaling resources based on demand. Serverless architectures, such as AWS Lambda and Azure Functions, enhance agility, reduce costs, and speed up the development process.

## Multi-Cloud and Hybrid Cloud

The adoption of multi-cloud and hybrid cloud strategies is trending. Companies are increasingly using multiple cloud providers to avoid vendor lock-in and improve resilience to cloud failure. Hybrid cloud solutions, which integrate private clouds (or on-premises data centres) with public clouds, offer the flexibility to run workloads in the most appropriate environment. Technologies, such as containerization, aim to facilitate seamless management and orchestration of applications across diverse cloud environments, making it easier for businesses to adopt multi-cloud or hybrid strategies.

## Edge Data Centres

Edge computing is also gaining momentum, driven by the need for low-latency data processing and real-time analytics. Low latency is achieved by building small data centres close to where they're needed. This is mission-critical for applications like the internet of things (IoT), autonomous vehicles, and smart cities. The internet is fast in human time but slow in computer time – it can take up to one hundred milliseconds to send a single message from London to New York – that's an age in computer time, and an interaction may require more than one message.

Cloud providers are increasingly offering edge solutions, such as AWS IoT Greengrass and Azure IoT Edge, to support these use cases. An often-quoted use case here is autonomous vehicles: to make split-second decisions – like braking to avoid a collision or swerving to accommodate road construction – a vehicle can't afford the delay of sending data back and forth to a distant central server. It needs an answer, and it needs it now.

## AI and ML Investments

Artificial intelligence and machine learning services are becoming integral to cloud offerings, enabling organizations to easily use advanced analytics and automation. Cloud platforms provide an array of tools and frameworks for developing, training, and deploying AI models, making it easier for businesses to incorporate AI into their operations.

## Blended Cloud

Cloud will become ubiquitous. It will be a utility in the same sense as water, gas, electricity, and the internet. The hard delineation that we now see between public, private, and industry-specific will dissipate and it will be a question of: where do you buy your resources? Ultimately, you will be able to switch cloud providers as easily as you can switch electricity providers. But there may be fewer choices, and don't hold your breath, as it were.

# CHAPTER SUMMARY

Cloud computing has revolutionized the way businesses acquire, use, and manage IT resources. Cloud offers flexibility, scalability, and the ability to drive digital transformation through the deployment of advanced technologies. The choice of cloud deployment model (public, private, or hybrid) will depend on an organization's specific needs, data sensitivity, and compliance requirements.

If you have non-cloud legacy systems, then moving to cloud is a major undertaking, impacting all aspects of the business – from legal and finance to HR, risk and compliance, and everything in the IT domain.

## Optimize Cloud Adoption for Your Organization

**Evaluate IT infrastructure:** assess your current IT setup to pinpoint where cloud computing can deliver the greatest benefits in cost savings, scalability, and agility.

**Create a cloud migration strategy:** develop a cloud migration path that aligns with business goals, considering factors like data sensitivity, regulatory compliance, and opex/capex costs.

**Select the right cloud models:** choose the appropriate cloud deployment (public, private, or hybrid) and service models (IaaS, PaaS, or SaaS), based on your organization's needs and workload characteristics.

**Train IT staff:** invest in training and upskilling your IT team to ensure they have the expertise to manage and secure cloud resources effectively. This is likely to be a significant investment.

**Implement strong security:** establish strong security measures and governance frameworks to protect sensitive data, comply with industry regulations, and use the shared responsibility model and security blueprints from cloud vendors.

# CHAPTER 4

# APIs, Big Data and Internet of Things

## The Powerful Enablers of Innovation Behind the Scenes

*What we need to do is always lean into the future; when the world changes around you and when it changes against you.*
*~ Jeff Bezos*

*Data is a precious thing and will last longer than the systems themselves.*
*~ Tim Berners-Lee*

*The Internet of Things has the potential to change the world, just as the internet did. Maybe even more so.*
*~ Kevin Ashton*

# Game Changers

In addition to the game changers of cloud and artificial intelligence, three other pieces of technology are helping to transform our world: APIs, big data and the IoT.* All three support a new, agile, fusion organization structure, a new way of working and a new way of developing and operating software solutions.

APIs allow smaller pieces of software, developed by smaller agile teams, to talk to each other in a standardized way. Big data captures the huge volumes of data generated by modern systems and allows us to gain insights and to train AI models. IoT recognizes that it makes no sense to transport all data to central repositories and that billions of chips in household appliances, vehicles, and other industrial devices are well placed to take on a lot of the work to be done

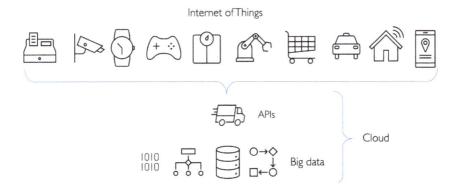

This chapter explores how these three technologies are driving significant change in our society and work environment.

---

\*   There are other high-impact technologies, such as blockchain, cryptocurrencies, robotics, 3D printing, smart contracts, quantum computing and more, but I've chosen these three as they are the core drivers of the fusion organization and interconnect with each other and with the organization architecturally.

# Application Programming Interfaces (APIs)

APIs play a crucial role in facilitating a distributed, fusion organization structure by enabling different software systems to communicate and collaborate seamlessly. APIs provide a standardized way for applications to interact with each other regardless of their underlying technology or platform. This allows systems developed in different programming languages, running on different operating systems, on different machines or in different locations, to work together. In other words, it makes it easy for your finance reporting system to access customer information, or your billing system to access an enterprise-wide forex calculator or for your system to access a third-party supplier's system.

Use of APIs encourages architectures where small (or at least not large, monolithic), autonomous services, built by small, autonomous teams, communicate through well-defined APIs.

## The Bezos Memo

Folklore has it that one day, Jeff Bezos, in a stroke of visionary zeal – or perhaps just frustrated by Amazon's IT architecture – issued a decree that would forever change how Amazon operated internally and, eventually, how companies all over the world thought about their software infrastructures. (Whether the memo ever existed is a myth of Arthurian proportions.[25]) It wasn't just a memo; it was more of a proclamation.

The directive was clear: all internal systems must be (re)structured to communicate through APIs, and every team must treat their services as if they might someday be accessed by external developers. This standardization of interfaces had profound organizational consequences: it meant that teams could build and deploy software with greater independence and therefore greater velocity as they were less constrained by waiting for another team to do work for them.

The memo's mandates were far-reaching. It insisted that every piece of data and functionality in Amazon's vast empire should be exposed as an API. This requirement meant that different Amazon services would not only need to operate independently but also interact seamlessly through well-defined interfaces.

The edict also stipulated that these APIs should be designed with the outside world in mind, turning every service into a potential standalone product that could be used by third parties.

The impact of this approach was profound. It shifted Amazon towards a microservices architecture long before the term was in vogue, enabling parts of the business to update and improve without waiting for a full overhaul of its systems – a bit like being able to remodel the kitchen without having to rebuild the whole house. This agility was a game changer. Furthermore, it laid the groundwork for what would become Amazon Web Services (AWS), turning what was essentially an internal infrastructure into one of the most dominant cloud platforms in the world.

By promoting this platform mindset, Bezos didn't just revolutionize Amazon; he inadvertently changed the trajectory of the software development industry. Companies began to see themselves not just as stores or service providers but as platforms that could support a whole ecosystem of products and services.

## How APIs Work

Application programming interfaces (APIs) serve as the conduits through which different software applications communicate and exchange data. At its core, an API defines the methods and data formats that developers should use when interacting with services, whether it be databases, web services, or even hardware.

One of the most popular types of API in web development is the RESTful API. This gets a bit techy, but bear with me. REST (representational state transfer) is an architectural style that uses standard internet protocols, making it ideal for communication across the internet.

So-called RESTful APIs are designed to work in a way where each request for information or action includes everything needed to understand and fulfil that request. In other words, the sending party asks the requested party to do some work and sends all the information that is required to get the work started. For example, "Pay this bill and here is the bank account number and the name of the payee", or "Give me the latest exchange rate buying dollars with yen", or "Give me the address details of client X".

This approach is incredibly powerful as it means that each party (or service) can work completely autonomously – services don't have to sit around waiting for more input to complete a request and they don't have to "remember" details from one request to another.

These services may reside on the same machine, in the same data centre or on different continents; they may be owned by the same enterprise, the same team or completely disparate organizations – that's the simplicity and the power of the internet and of APIs.

# Big Data

Big data refers to extremely large datasets that are too complex to process and analyse using traditional data processing techniques. It encompasses the collection, storage, analysis, and visualization of data.

As businesses increasingly interact with customers online and automate operations with digital technologies, the volume, variety, and velocity (the three Vs) of data they generate grows exponentially. The data is coming from capturing every detail of every transaction, interaction and API call executed using a computer. We don't just capture the basic data; we capture the data about the data (metadata). We know the route a consumer has taken to arrive at a particular decision on a website, how long it took, what flavour of browser was used, the timestamp, the location, perhaps even the weather conditions and forecast.

APIs provide the means to feed the big data beast's insatiable appetite and IoT devices generate a tremendous amount of real-time data from sensors embedded in various devices across different sectors – from industrial machines to wearable technology.

Some of this data is functionally required to execute a request, track progress, or monitor performance; other data is required to meet audit or regulatory requirements, yet more is for statistical analysis and even more because we think we might need the data at some point in the future for some as yet unforeseen need – a kind of FOMO data retention policy.

Cloud provides the infrastructure necessary for storing and processing big data. It offers scalable resources on demand, which are essential for handling the immense volume and velocity without the need for organizations to invest in their own data centres. Cloud services also offer advanced analytics tools that can quickly derive insights from large datasets stored in the cloud.

Big data is one of those umbrella terms that's not quite as easy to define as an API. In fact, big data is, for the most part, more of a big yawn. But it's the capability that processing massive amounts of data brings that makes it interesting. Big data isn't a new type of database or query language, it's more an overall principle or architecture for managing and utilizing the massive amount of data we collect.

## Real-World Examples

In the world of retail, big data is revolutionizing how companies interact with their customers. By analysing extensive customer purchase histories and online shopping behaviours, retailers can offer personalized product recommendations and optimize their inventory to meet demand more precisely.

In healthcare, the application of big data is transformative. Hospitals are using this technology to predict patient admissions and enhance diagnostic processes. By recognizing patterns in medical imaging and analysing patient data over time, healthcare providers can offer more accurate diagnoses and tailor treatments to individual patient needs, significantly improving patient outcomes.

### Bosch Leverages IoT, Big Data and AI[26]

Bosch employs AI, IoT and big data in its manufacturing processes to enhance efficiency and achieve near-zero defects. At their Bamberg plant, AI systems analyse data from over 1,400 production lines, identifying quality issues in real time and optimizing production workflows. This integration of AI with sensors and data analytics allows Bosch to detect and address anomalies immediately, significantly reducing downtime and ensuring high product quality.
The AI system processes millions of data points daily, transforming manufacturing into a highly automated and precise operation. With AI, Bosch can make data-driven decisions, streamline operations, and maintain a competitive edge in the industry.

The finance sector has found a powerful ally in big data for enhancing security and operational integrity. Financial institutions analyse vast amounts of transaction data in real time to detect and prevent fraud.

In the transportation sector, big data is key to solving urban congestion issues. Traffic management systems analyse data from numerous sources to optimize traffic flow in real time, adjusting traffic light sequences and providing route suggestions to reduce congestion and enhance urban mobility.

# The IoT: Connecting the Physical and Digital Worlds

The internet of things, or IoT, represents a significant shift in how we interact with the physical world around us. Like big data, it's more of a concept built on top of the existing rails of the internet, supplemented by communication protocols such as 5G, Bluetooth, Zigbee and Z-Wave.

This technology connects everyday objects (kitchen appliances, heating thermostats, bathroom scales, industrial equipment, vehicles etc.) to the internet, allowing them to send and receive data. The real power of IoT lies in its ability to turn physical actions (triggered or fed by sensors) into rich data, which can then be analysed to optimize processes, provide insights, and predict future events.

IoT technology is transforming various sectors by providing real-time insights and automated control over a myriad of operations – feeding big data collections and cloud usage in the process.

In manufacturing, IoT devices can monitor equipment performance and predict failures before they occur, minimizing downtime and maintenance costs. In agriculture, sensors can track soil moisture and nutrients, helping farmers apply water and fertilizers more efficiently to increase crop yield.

Your smartwatch, smart ring and fitness tracker are connected to your smartphone, which is connected to a cloud provider: hundreds of millions of devices generating massive volumes of data points per day about heart rate, location, sport metrics, and more. Your bathroom scales may be connected to your health app. Your smart thermostats, smart locks, home security systems, smart speakers, and appliances might be remotely controlled and monitored from wherever you are in the world. For services funded by advertising, this provides a treasure trove of insights for personalization. For others, it offers insights to create better products and predict market behaviour.

Smart cities are made possible by the convergence of IoT and 5G to improve urban living. Smart traffic lights and streetlamps collect and respond to real-time data, reducing congestion and energy usage. Public safety improves through connected security cameras and emergency response systems that act swiftly based on continuous data streams. Municipal services become more responsive as IoT sensors monitor infrastructure like bridges and roads, predicting maintenance needs before breakdowns occur.

Healthcare, transport, gas, and electricity usage, smart lighting systems, home automation… there are a lot of devices out there.

## 5G as an Enabler of Advanced IoT Applications

The rollout of 5G technology is turbocharging IoT capabilities. With its faster speeds, lower latency, and higher capacity, 5G makes it possible to scale up IoT applications. 5G enables more devices to connect and communicate simultaneously, supports the transmission of large amounts of data without lag, and allows for the deployment of critical and complex applications that require real-time operations.

As companies continue to explore the potential of IoT, the integration of 5G will unlock even greater possibilities, marking a new era of innovation in how we interact with and manage our physical world.

# CHAPTER SUMMARY

APIs, big data, and the internet of things (IoT) are transforming the way organizations operate and innovate. These technologies are enabling the creation of agile, distributed, and data-driven systems in fusion organizations that can adapt to rapidly changing business needs.

By using these technologies, companies can gain valuable insights, optimize processes, and deliver personalized experiences to customers.

## Harness APIs, Big Data, and IoT for Growth

**API strategy development:** create an API architecture and strategy to ensure seamless communication and collaboration across systems and services, both internally and with external partners.

**Invest in big data:** build a big data infrastructure with analytics capabilities to leverage the vast amounts of data from digital interactions and IoT devices.

**Adopt IoT technologies:** utilize IoT to bridge the physical and digital divide, enabling real-time monitoring, predictive maintenance, and automation of various processes and operations.

**Encourage innovation:** foster a culture of innovation and experimentation, urging teams to use APIs, big data, and IoT to develop valuable new products, services, and business models.

**Ensure security and privacy:** implement strong security and privacy measures to protect sensitive data and maintain trust, recognizing that the proliferation of APIs, big data, and IoT devices increases the potential cybersecurity vulnerabilities.

# CHAPTER 5

# The New Digital Executives

New Structures. New Roles. Aligning and Inspiring Leadership.

*Clearly AI is going to win. How people are going to adjust is a fascinating problem.*
*~ Daniel Kahneman*

*Never doubt that a small group of committed individuals can change the world.*
*Indeed, it is the only thing that ever has.*
*~ Margaret Mead*

*Finding good players is easy. Getting them to play as a team is another story.*
*~ Casey Stengel*

# The Senior Executive Team

Digital transformation and AI are changing the shape of organizations and the structure and responsibilities of leadership teams. These are uncharted waters and leaders need to have a sense of purpose, a strong moral compass, and an ability to navigate a storm.

Let's start with a look at the changing scope and roles of the senior executive team. This assumes that there is such a thing that can be referred to as a "senior team" in an ultra-flat, AI-driven fusion organization. However, having glanced at where we're going, let's start from the relative familiarity and comfort of where we are.

The senior team used to be a clutch of individuals at the top of a hierarchy. It can now be tens of individuals. A compelling example of this evolution is seen in the operational model adopted by NVIDIA's CEO, Jensen Huang. He has fifty-five direct reports; they all get paid the same salary; he has no one-to-ones unless requested and does no annual performance reviews.[27] Huang's model suggests a broader trend where AI and automation are not only reshaping the responsibilities within the C-suite but also redefining leadership dynamics. Technology facilitates a more fluid, dynamic approach to leadership and decision-making.

The senior leadership roles can be broadly divided into programme-based roles and permanent roles. Whether these roles report directly into the CEO or to another executive is a question of how much authority or political influence (internal or external) the role may require in getting results and will reflect the strategic, cultural and tactical priorities of the firm.

The programme-based roles may have a tenure of a few years and are intended to effect large-scale change in a short time period. Fixed roles are permanent and are responsible for defining and executing the firm's strategy for the longer term. My exploration below is by no means exhaustive but aims to highlight the changing roles of some of the more familiar abbreviations found in our enterprises.

# Chief Executive Officer (CEO)

The CEO's role is impacted fundamentally, requiring a more direct involvement with technology, organizational flexibility, and resilience. The impact of technology across all aspects of the business – from operating model, product offering, customer support, to HR and finance – is such that the CEO needs to update what they pay attention to, with whom they spend their time and what topics are on the board agenda.

This shift highlights a strategic pivot where digital transformation is viewed as a critical component of the overall business strategy, necessitating direct oversight from the highest executive level.

Top of the to-do list are six focus areas:

## Governance, Leadership and a Digital Culture

Leadership is crucial in driving digital transformation. The CEO needs to champion digital initiatives. This requires a clear governance structure that promotes agility, risk-taking with risk management, and a collaborative working environment.

CEOs must not only endorse, but actively drive, the adoption of digital technologies, demonstrating commitment from the top. It's important for CEOs to establish clear roles and responsibilities that align with digital goals that support the enterprise mission.

Against a background of uncertainty about the future, the CEO must communicate a clear digital vision throughout the organization, ensuring that all levels of the company understand and are engaged with the digital transformation journey.

## Values and Ethics

As the highest-ranking executive, the CEO sets the tone for the organization's values and ethical standards. They must ensure that AI technologies are developed and deployed responsibly, prioritizing transparency, fairness, and accountability. This involves implementing good governance frameworks, fostering a culture of ethical awareness, and promoting continuous education on AI ethics among employees.

The CEO should also engage with stakeholders, including customers, regulators, and industry peers, to align AI practices with societal expectations and legal requirements. By championing ethical AI use, the CEO not only mitigates risks but also builds trust and enhances the company's reputation in the marketplace.

### Lead Transformations and HR Consequences

CEOs need to champion agile and DevOps practices within their organizations. This includes handling the HR challenges of the ensuing disruption. Transformation means initiating and supporting shifts to more agile and collaborative work processes. It involves organizing smaller, cross-functional teams that work on short project cycles and continuously refine their outputs based on real-time feedback.

### Develop Digital Skills in the Workforce

CEOs must ensure their workforce is competent in digital skills. This action involves overseeing training programmes, hiring for digital expertise, and fostering a culture that values continuous learning and adaptability.

### Manage Technological Risks and Cybersecurity

As technology becomes more embedded in every aspect of business, CEOs must also become adept at managing its risks. This includes implementing strong cybersecurity measures, ensuring data privacy compliance, and addressing ethical concerns related to AI, such as bias in decision-making processes.

### Drive Customer-Centric Innovation

Utilizing AI, CEOs need to spearhead the development of new, personalized customer experiences. This could mean using data analytics to tailor products and services or employing machine learning to improve customer service interactions.

# Chief Information Officer (CIO)

The CIO has traditionally been in charge of managing an organization's information and data assets. The CIO often works on enhancing business processes through technology solutions and collaborates with various departments to ensure that technology supports the company's objectives. The role is typically less technology oriented than the chief technology officer (CTO) role and more organizationally inward facing. However, as technology becomes more deeply integrated into every aspect of the business, the responsibilities once held by the CIO are now being distributed across the organization.

The question is: in a highly distributed fusion organization, do you need a CIO?

Most firms will need a central authority with a seat on the board who is responsible for technology – possibly (or probably) including digital transformation and AI, but certainly including enterprise-wide technology policies, technology strategy, and the underlying enablers, such as infrastructure.

In fusion organizations, where IT is no longer a siloed department but rather an integral part of every business unit, the management of information and data assets is no longer the sole responsibility of the CIO. This decentralization of IT management has led to a paradigm shift in the role of the CIO, with many of their traditional responsibilities being absorbed by other business leaders and teams.

As a result, the CIO faces a bit of an identity crisis. With a significant portion of their job description no longer relevant in the context of a fusion organization, the question arises: what is the future of the CIO role? This is a particularly challenging question given the extensive ecosystem that has developed around the three letters of the CIO title, including publications, events, awards, and educational programmes.

The CIO title has become deeply ingrained in the fabric of the IT industry, making it difficult to envision a future without it. However, as organizations continue to evolve and adapt to the demands of the digital age, it is becoming increasingly clear that the CIO role, as it has been traditionally defined, may no longer be relevant.

Ultimately, the focus should be on the responsibilities and functions of the role, rather than the specific title. Whether an organization chooses to retain the CIO title or create a new one, the key is to ensure that the role is aligned with the needs and goals of the organization.

There are a number of options available for the CIO, for example:

- Keep the title but change the "I" to "Innovation" (Chief Innovation Officer). By transforming the role into a chief innovation officer, the focus shifts from managing information systems to driving innovation throughout the organization. Some organizations are blending the role into the hybrid chief innovation and technology officer (CITO).

- Transition to a chief digital officer or chief transformation officer role (see section below).
- Blend with the chief product officer (CPO) or CTO role and rebrand as CPIO or CITO.
- A governance role: in this capacity, the transformed CIO would oversee the governance of all IT and digital processes across the organization. Responsibilities could include governance frameworks and ensuring compliance with internal and external regulations.
- Speak to HR about a career move: for some, the situation may mean that their skills could be better utilized in different roles, either within the organization or externally.

For our discussion in this book, I'll use the term CTO to describe the senior executive who is responsible for the technology within the organization. More on the role of the CTO later in the chapter.

# Enterprise Architect (EA)

If the role of the CIO is evolving, that of the EA is gaining in strategic importance.

Enterprise architecture seeks to strategically align all systems and processes horizontally and vertically in a business. Horizontally across divisions, business units, and departments, and vertically from the organization's purpose and strategy to the choice of technology upon which the business systems run.

Enterprise architecture is about ensuring that technology investments are not just tactical but drive long-term value. Enterprise architecture provides a blueprint for future growth and efficiency, helping organizations streamline operations and reduce costs through improved technology integration and governance.

The EA is far from being a purely technological role. The EA's skills and competencies should include strong business acumen, communication skills, and the ability to translate complex technical concepts into business language. EA's must be able to engage with stakeholders at all levels of the organization, from senior executives to front-line employees, to understand their needs and challenges and design architectures that can support them.

Given the level of influence that the enterprise architect should be allowed, the role should report at a very senior level in the organization. The strategic importance of enterprise architecture means that they must have direct access to the highest levels of decision-making. Reporting to senior leadership, such as the CEO, COO or CTO ensures that the EA can effectively advocate for architectural decisions that align with the company's long-term vision and goals.

This senior reporting structure enables the EA to influence major business and technology initiatives, ensuring that the architectural roadmap is integrated into the overall strategic plan. It also allows the EA to facilitate cross-departmental collaboration, breaking down silos and fostering a unified approach to digital transformation and innovation.

More on this important role later in the Architecting the Enterprise chapter.

# Chief Transformation/Digital/AI Officer

Programme-based C-level roles such as the chief transformation officer (CTrO), chief data officer (CDO) and chief AI officer (CAIO) are specifically focused on driving change within an organization. These roles are responsible for spearheading organizational change by identifying strategic opportunities for process improvement, optimizing operations, and leading initiatives to adapt to evolving market conditions.

They work across departments to facilitate the adoption of new strategies and technologies, fostering innovation and growth. Typically, these roles are internally focused and programme-based.

# Chief Technology Officer (CTO)

The CTO brings technology vision to the organization. They are responsible for aligning technology initiatives with business goals and objectives. In a world where technology and business are virtually inseparable, having a CTO at the helm ensures that a firm's technology strategy is in harmony with its purpose.

Depending on the type of CTO and the scale and maturity of the organization, the enterprise architect and chief information security officer may also report into the CTO. For many SMEs, this configuration of roles provides a central governance point for providing common guard rails and standards across the organization.

More on this pivotal role in the separate The Chief Technology Officer chapter.

# Chief Information Security Officer (CISO)

The CISO is responsible for the development and execution of an organization's information security strategy. This includes identifying, assessing, and mitigating security risks to protect the organization's digital assets and data.

This role involves developing and implementing security policies, conducting regular security audits, ensuring compliance with regulatory requirements, and leading incident response efforts in the event of a cyberattack.

In terms of reporting lines, the same applies for the CISO as the enterprise architect – they should report as high into the organization as makes sense for the context. This reporting structure ensures that cybersecurity considerations are integrated into the organization's overall strategic planning and decision-making processes. It also emphasizes the importance of cybersecurity at the highest levels of the organization, providing the CISO with the authority and resources needed to effectively safeguard the organization's information assets.

A recent report[28] found that almost 50% of CISOs report to the CEO. Apart from the CEO route, the CISO may also report to the COO, chief risk officer (CRO), or other C-title, depending on the type of business. For smaller organizations, the CISO may report into the CTO, or the responsibilities may even be blended into the CTO role.

# Chief Financial Officer (CFO)

The CFO's responsibility has become a multifaceted role, going far beyond being a financial steward – making sure the firm's balance sheet, cash flow and P&L are in order. The CFO must now embrace advanced digitization of all the firm's assets. They drive data-based decision-making and may also be responsible for risk and compliance. The modern CFO is expected to understand the impact of technology on financial performance and navigate a path through increasingly complex regulatory requirements.

# Chief Human Resources Officer (CHRO)

The CHRO plays a key role in embracing new technology and new organization structures to enable agility within the workforce. The importance of this role can hardly be overstated. Layered on top of working from home (WfH); diversity, equity, and inclusion (DEI); and the restructuring of whole organizations to form agile teams, they are now faced with the workforce impact of AI.

The CHRO is responsible for aligning HR strategies with digital tools and systems that support agile team structures and practices across the organization. This includes developing an HR roadmap that is tightly aligned with the technology transformation roadmap to ensure people are recruited, trained, and retained in a timely fashion.

In a world with a chronic shortage of skilled IT, cybersecurity and AI engineers, being an HR recruiter is a big job.

# Chief Risk (and Compliance) Officer (CRO)

The CRO often includes regulatory compliance and may be referred to as the CRCO. No industry is completely free from regulation in some form, but the role of the CRO in many industries is, like that of the CFO and CHRO, undergoing substantial change across healthcare, technology, social media, privacy, AI, data management, and more.

The multitude of regulations impacts most (if not all) of a firm's disciplines and departments, making CRO a key team player in ensuring the organization not only does the right thing, but can also demonstrate and evidence that it's doing so.

# Chief Product Officer (CPO)

The CPO is the voice of the customer in product development. The CPO in a modern agile DevOps context is a visionary leader, deeply attuned to market dynamics and customer needs. Their responsibilities encompass strategic product planning, ensuring seamless integration of technology through close collaboration with the chief technology officer.

The CPO's agile mindset drives iterative product development, emphasizing rapid prototyping and a learn-fast approach. Effective cross-functional collaboration is a hallmark, fostering unity between product, development, and other teams.

# The Non-Executive Board

Non-executive boards (or supervisory or oversight boards) do not have a lot of time. They typically meet a few times each year to oversee the performance of the executive directors – not least in terms of compliance, financial health, ethics and long-term strategy. The size of both the opportunity and the threat of digitization and AI means these items need to be on their agenda.

Just as finance and human resources often warrant dedicated subcommittees to address their complexity and significance to the business, IT and AI similarly merit focused oversight. Establishing a board subcommittee dedicated to IT and AI can provide the specialized attention required to navigate these rapidly changing fields effectively. Such a specialized subcommittee may be charged with several critical responsibilities, such as:

Strategic Alignment: Ensuring that digital and AI strategies align with the overall business strategy, driving growth and innovation while managing risk.

Technology Investment and Value: Assessing the return on investment for technology initiatives, ensuring that digital transformation efforts deliver tangible business value and maintain financial health.

Cybersecurity and Data Governance: Monitoring the organization's cybersecurity posture and data governance practices to protect against data breaches, intellectual property theft, and compliance violations.

Ethical and Responsible AI Use: Overseeing the ethical deployment of AI technologies, including considerations around data privacy, bias in AI models, and the social impact of automation.

Talent and Culture: Guiding the organization in cultivating the talent and culture needed.

# CHAPTER SUMMARY

Digital transformation and AI are fundamentally reshaping organizational structures and leadership roles, requiring leaders to navigate uncharted waters.

This chapter explored the evolving responsibilities within the senior leadership team. It highlighted how the team as a whole, and the leaders individually, must adapt in a fusion organization where technology and business strategies are deeply integrated. The creation of a fusion organization may signal a fundamental shift of the CIO role as we've known it for the last few decades.

## Drive Digital Transformation and AI Adoption

**Redefine leadership roles:** adjust leadership responsibilities to meet the demands of digital transformation and AI, ensuring every executive understands their role in driving technological change.

**Establish appropriate governance:** create a governance structure that emphasizes agility, risk management, and collaboration, with the CEO actively promoting AI and digital initiatives, and a clear vision throughout the organization.

**Develop digital skills:** invest in workforce training, strategic hiring, and fostering a culture of continuous learning and adaptability to build essential digital skills.

**Enhance cybersecurity and ethics:** implement strong cybersecurity measures and ensure compliance with data privacy regulations, addressing ethical concerns like AI bias in decision-making processes.

**Create an IT and AI subcommittee:** form a dedicated board subcommittee to align strategies, oversee technology investments, monitor cybersecurity and data governance, ensure ethical AI use, and guide talent and culture development.

# CHAPTER 6

# The Chief Technology Officer

Centre Stage or Eye of the Storm?

*Feeling unprepared for technical disruption? A well-structured role for the chief technology officer is a first line of defence.*
*~ McKinsey*

*Work takes on new meaning when you feel you are pointed in the right direction. Otherwise, it's just a job, and life is too short for that.*
*~ Tim Cook*

# A Defining Factor for Business Success

The ability to leverage the power of technology effectively has become a defining factor for business success, and this is where the role of a chief technology officer (CTO) is centre stage - or, perhaps, in the eye of the storm.

The velocity of technology change is increasing, but so too is its amplitude. New hardware, software, tooling, and services stream onto the market on a daily basis. Keeping up requires an ability to context-switch rapidly between the micro and the macro – to grasp the detail (or at least the potential impact of the detail) and to understand the context. Arguably, this applies to all executives, but the CTO is faced with the unique and relentless challenge of the speed of innovation.

If a part of the role of the CFO is to avoid earnings surprises, then a part of the CTO role is to avoid technology surprises. Missing a key innovation (e.g. mobile, or AI), or failing to engineer systems to properly reflect business priorities (e.g. an outage or security breach), may not only cost the CTO their job, but it may also deliver an existential threat to the organization.

The CTO brings technology vision to the organization. They are responsible for aligning technology initiatives with business goals and objectives. In a world where technology and business are virtually inseparable, having a CTO at the helm ensures that a firm's technology strategy is in harmony with its purpose.

As a leader, the CTO provides direction, ensuring that all aspects of IT are not just a supporting function but an integral driver of innovation and success. The CTO is a champion of innovation: exploring emerging technologies, trends, and opportunities that can give the organization a competitive edge. They lead the research and development efforts, enabling the creation of new (technology) products, services, and solutions that meet the changing needs of customers and the organization.

The recommendations and choices the CTO makes will have far-reaching effects on the future of an organization. Despite much tech industry standardization, big-ticket decisions almost always entail a technology lock-in, and usually a supplier lock-in. Your choice of cloud supplier and programming language are typical examples here. Today's technology landscape is vast and intricate, encompassing a multitude of tools, platforms, and systems. The tech industry players seek strategic advantage by creating an ecosystem that increases switching costs. Apple, Microsoft, Google, Amazon, and others excel at this ecosystem construction. The CTO must manage these complex technology ecosystems, ensuring that the organization's technology infrastructure is efficient, secure, and scalable. They make critical decisions regarding technology investments, architecture, and partnerships.

# The CTO Agenda

Getting the most out of IT is about six highly integrated areas of business technology leadership. These areas form the essential agenda for the CTO and the backbone of any IT strategy. Some of these areas will be shared responsibility with other disciplines – such as HR, Risk, Compliance, or Legal.

The six aspects are: People, Process & Policy, Technology, Architecture, Cybersecurity, and Legal & Compliance. Properly blended with leadership, creativity, persistence, and engineering talent, these six elements will provide a blueprint for creating incredible product to delight customers.

# People

First and foremost in the job description is people and organization, encompassing all the leadership characteristics of creating great teams of people and building a strong digital culture, not only within the IT community but across the whole enterprise.

The success of any digital initiative hinges on the quality and capabilities of the people involved. As such, the CTO must be a strong leader who can build and inspire high-performing teams. This starts with attracting top talent from diverse backgrounds, including software development, data analytics, cloud computing, AI, and other emerging technologies.

We'll explore the leadership styles of the CTO later in this chapter.

# Process & Policy

Or "how we do business around here". For a CTO, process and policy are crucial as they provide a structured approach to managing an organization's technology portfolio of assets and services. Clear processes ensure that technology tasks are executed efficiently, consistently, and in alignment with business goals. Policies establish standards for security, compliance, and governance, mitigating risks and safeguarding intellectual property.

There are two broad and interwoven areas here:

**The policy framework:** selection of a standard for a structured framework designed to systematically develop, implement, and manage policies and processes, ensuring consistency, security, compliance, and alignment with strategic objectives.

**The agile methodology:** selection and implementation of an agile software development and operations framework.

Implementing effective processes is critical to ensuring that the organization's technology function runs smoothly, efficiently, and meets compliance and (external) audit requirements.

Creative IT people are not always keen on this part of their work, and it can be misconstrued as being an academic exercise to please the auditors. But done well, it is both good for the business and for meeting audit requirements. Done well, it creates guard rails and guidelines within which autonomy can be maximized. Done well, it outlines how we design, build, deploy and operate IT products; how we serve customers; maintain a reliable infrastructure; how we do cybersecurity; what we do when things don't go as planned; how we monitor and measure what's going on; how we train our staff, and more.

| | |
|---|---|
| • IT Strategy | • Business Continuity & |
| • Governance and Organization | Disaster Recovery |
| • Architecture | • Physical Security |
| • Software Engineering | • Data Protection |
| • Asset Management | • Metrics and Reporting |
| • Cybersecurity | • Network Security |
| • Incident Management | • Product Development |
| • Identity and Access Management | • Third Party Management |

Examples of domains in a structured policy framework

Establishing a policy framework is a significant endeavour, and it's an ongoing process – policies and processes must evolve as the environment changes. Despite seeming daunting, it's more manageable than it appears. For instance, a bank might require extensive policy documentation, while a start-up can get by with just a few pages. The detail level depends on risk tolerance: a start-up with ten employees might opt for minimal formal security training, whereas a bank with fifty thousand employees must make substantial investments.

However, help is at hand in the form of industry standard frameworks. The most commonly used are:

- **ITIL (Information Technology Infrastructure Library):** provides best practices for IT service management, focusing on aligning IT services with the needs of the business and improving efficiency and service delivery.
- **COBIT (Control Objectives for Information and Related Technologies):** offers a complete framework for governance and management of enterprise IT, helping ensure that IT is aligned with business goals, risks are managed, and value is maximized.
- **TOGAF (The Open Group Architecture Framework):** a framework for enterprise architecture that provides a structured approach for designing, planning, implementing, and governing enterprise information architecture.
- **Agile and DevOps:** there are a variety of flavours here, from highly structured to more loosely structured. More on these later in the Developing Great Software chapter.

- **ISO/IEC 27001:** a standard for information security management systems (ISMS) that helps organizations protect their information assets, ensure data integrity, and comply with regulatory requirements.

All the standards can be of use but making the right selection of (a subset of) one or two will help develop a structure and a roadmap for building and maintaining IT health.

# Technology

Selecting and implementing the right technologies and partners is absolutely critical for the CTO. Making a wrong choice can lead to drawn-out, time-wasting, money-draining, and energy-sapping projects with a frustrating opportunity cost. The pressure is often on to make quick decisions – from business stakeholders who may need to reduce costs or get a product to market, but often from the engineering teams in the IT domain. Software engineers are often presented with a dizzying array of third-party solutions to solve any particular problem – be it a technology problem or a business challenge – but you can't have them all.

This is a trade-off game primarily driven by the value added for the business, so you can't please all the people all the time. Equally, there may not be enough time to carry out a full evaluation of all the options, run pilots, carry out due diligence on the suppliers and examine all the pros and cons. In selecting technology partners, the CTO must carefully assess the capabilities and track record of potential vendors and service providers. These partners may provide valuable expertise and resources to support the organization's digital initiatives, but they must be carefully vetted to ensure that they are financially sound, have the necessary skills and experience, and are a good cultural fit. The CTO has to balance all these, often conflicting, requirements and make a choice – and sometimes maybe take an informed gamble, or judgment call.

The CTO must take a proactive approach to technology scouting and staying up to date with the latest developments. They must evaluate the potential impact of new technologies on the organization's industry and business model and make informed decisions about which ones to invest in.

Once technology partners have been selected, the CTO must work closely with them to ensure that their solutions are properly integrated into the organization's overall technology stack. This may involve customizing or configuring products to meet specific business needs, establishing service-level agreements and performance metrics, and ensuring that data is properly secured and governed.

The CTO must ensure that the organization's technology stack is flexible, modular, and scalable enough to support future growth and innovation. By creating a technology foundation that is nimble and adaptable, the CTO can help the organization to respond quickly to new opportunities and challenges.

And all the tech choices made must fit into the overall architecture.

# Architecture

The technology architecture of an organization is the foundation upon which all of its digital initiatives are built. As such, it is critical that the CTO ensures that this architecture is properly aligned both horizontally and vertically across the organization.

Horizontal alignment refers to the integration and interoperability of different systems across the organization's various business processes and value chain. This includes everything from the applications and databases used by different departments to the networks and infrastructure that support them. The CTO should ensure that these components are properly integrated and can exchange data and functionality seamlessly.

Vertical alignment refers to the alignment of the technology architecture with the organization's overall purpose and strategy, from the highest-level business goals down to the lowest-level technical details. This requires the CTO to have a deep understanding of the organization's mission, values, and objectives, and to translate these into a technology strategy that supports them.

To achieve proper alignment, the CTO must work closely with other business leaders to understand their needs and requirements, and to ensure that the technology architecture is designed to support them. This may involve conducting regular strategy sessions and workshops, where business and technology leaders can collaborate to define the organization's digital vision and roadmap.

Once the high-level strategy is defined, the CTO must then work with their team to translate it into a more detailed technology architecture. This may involve creating reference architectures, design patterns, and other technical artifacts that provide a common language and framework for development teams to work within.

# Cybersecurity

Cybersecurity means securing the company's digital assets against loss, theft, and damage, including cyber threats, data breaches, regulatory requirements, and any form of disaster. In security, the CTO will work very closely with the CISO as many of the responsibilities are shared. (The CISO may in practice report to the CTO.)

This area includes implementing security measures to protect against a wide array of cyber threats, such as hacking attempts, phishing attacks, and malware infections, which can compromise sensitive company information and disrupt operations.

The CTO must ensure that the organization is equipped with the right technology, such as firewalls, intrusion detection systems, continuous monitoring, and encryption technologies to prevent damage to the company's assets.

Regular security audits and vulnerability assessments are essential to identify and mitigate potential weaknesses in the system. The CTO, together with the CISO, CRO and all business leaders, must develop and enforce security protocols and policies, ensuring that all employees are trained in best practices for cybersecurity.

We'll explore cybersecurity in greater detail in the Cybersecurity Threats and Opportunities chapter.

# Legal & Compliance

In recent years, governments and regulatory bodies around the world have introduced a wide range of new technology regulations and legislation aimed at protecting consumer privacy, ensuring data security, and promoting fair competition in the digital economy.

To ensure compliance with these and other external and internal regulations, guidelines and policies, the CTO must work closely with legal and compliance teams to understand the specific requirements and obligations that apply to the organization. This may involve conducting regular audits and assessments of the organization's technology systems and processes to identify any gaps or vulnerabilities that could lead to non-compliance.

One of the key challenges in this area is the fact that technology regulations and legislation are constantly evolving and changing. As new technologies emerge and new risks are identified, governments, regulators, and industry bodies are likely to introduce new requirements and standards that organizations must comply with. The CTO must therefore stay up to date with the latest developments and be prepared to adapt and evolve the organization's compliance strategies as needed.

To help manage this complexity, many organizations are turning to specialized compliance management software and tools, which can automate many of the processes involved in monitoring and reporting on compliance. The CTO must evaluate these tools and determine which ones are best suited to the organization's specific needs and requirements.

In the event of a compliance breach or violation, the CTO is often at the eye of the storm. This may involve conducting investigations, notifying relevant authorities and stakeholders, and implementing corrective actions to prevent similar incidents from occurring in the future.

# The CTO Leadership Styles

What characteristics should a CTO have? What type of CTO best fits your organization? How will they best work with an existing executive team?

My intention here is not to put people into boxes with labels, but to provide personality patterns and skill set profiles for reflection or for discussion about shaping the function of the CTO and the technology leadership team. Tech is a team sport, and a healthy mix of personalities creates a strong team.

There are four styles of CTO: I call them the "chairman", the "networker", the "banker", and the "professional".[29]

In general, we see these four leadership styles in all roles and organizations, as I discussed in my previous book.[3] Everyone has something of all the styles. A CTO will lean towards a preferred style and possess a particular skill set and background experience. No style is inherently better than any other. Similarly, within each style, the good, the bad and the great CTOs can be found.

I've used the labels of "chairman", "networker", "banker", and "professional" as shorthand. It's clearly not black and white – all CTOs (indeed all leaders) will have a blend of the traits in how they work.

| | Smaller ← Organization Size → Larger | |
|---|---|---|
| **Higher**<br>Organizational Complexity<br>**Lower** | **Banker**<br>Realistic<br>Decisive<br>Stable | **Chairman**<br>Supportive<br>Coalition-builder<br>Visionary |
| | **Professional**<br>Intelligent<br>Self-reliant<br>Thoughtful | **Networker**<br>Relationship-builder<br>Communicative<br>Charismatic |

The style of the CTO and the culture of the technology team will reflect those of the organization as a whole but will also impact how the organization behaves, how it defines its strategy, achieves its goals, how innovative it is, and how much risk it is prepared to accept.

All good CTOs will have a mix of "chairman", "networker", "banker", and "professional" in their profile.

# The Chairman CTO

The chairman understands the process of consulting with others and building consensus. They are your best supporter. They are visionary, but their vision of the future is a shared one and is based on mutual understanding. They have a strong character and are self-confident. They understand people, can listen well, and motivate others through helping them realize their potential. They understand how to bring the potentially diverse parts of an organization together into a coherent whole. They are a master at the political game and can build teams and foster trust.

The chairman will talk to each member of their team individually when necessary to avoid and resolve conflict. They will also bring the team together when necessary and chair meetings to good effect. The chairman CTO is often a good representative of their group to the outside world, presenting a unified image of the organization.

The chairman may need to learn to "chill" a little and let go on occasion. They need to be realistic about what is achievable. They must temper their tendency for consensus with decisiveness.

The chairman CTO is good at orchestrating major transformation and keeping a watchful eye to ensure that all the arrows are facing in the same direction – that everybody is aligned and engaged in the undertaking. They may initiate new projects, but the original idea is likely to come from an external source.

# The Networker CTO

The network is technically competent but not an expert. The networker is an excellent communicator. They prefer face-to-face communication as they can then use all their communicative powers and can better gauge the reaction of others. They are empathic and will quickly and intuitively lock on to the thinking style of others. Their natural language skills are also useful in written communication – from a brief email to an eloquent formal letter or document. The networker is charming, makes friends easily, is sociable, easy-going, and charismatic.

The networker fits well into a strongly distributed IT organization and will bring parties together across (political) divides. This means the networker brings useful skills in building and maintaining a team where the IT staff are embedded across an organization.

In digital transformation campaigns, the networker CTO is a great communicator and motivator. The networker typically excels at initiating change and is good at generating ideas. Follow-through and execution may not be their strong points, however.

The networker will have little problem in convincing others that change is necessary. Their optimism and charisma will encourage others to follow.

# The Banker CTO

In contrast to the networker, the banker is assertive, serious, realistic and strong-minded. The banker will have no problem in taking decisions, as long as the parameters within which they must work are clear. The banker excels at execution and makes a great operational manager. They are solid and trustworthy, and people always know where they stand with them. The banker is generally stable and can be relied upon to do what they say they're going to do.

The banker is less of a technology expert and will typically have a strong tech team to support them. The banker can be found typically in organizations where the emphasis of the CTO is on operational excellence and regulatory adherence. In such a setting, an element of flair and creativity is needed from, say, the CPO to provide innovation and balance.

The banker CTO is great at execution but less talented at innovation. Once convinced of the need for a project, they will be dogged in their determination to see it through. The realistic side of the banker's personality will ensure that change is achievable and that targets are met. The banker is an excellent type to have on board to ensure execution.

# The Professional CTO

The professional is the prototypical tech CTO. Most likely educated and trained in software engineering, computer science, or AI. A professional type of CTO is more often found in start-ups or smaller organizations where a hands-on approach to technology may be more important than general management skills.

The professional feels comfortable with technology, architecture, and process but may feel less so with soft skills, such as people management.

The professional is a clever individualist. Their colleagues accept them as a leader due to their superior knowledge and experience. The professional is intelligent and thrives on intellectual challenges. Run of the mill is boring. They like to think through problems and arrive at smart solutions. They have no problem working alone or with teams of like-minded people. The professional is not always easily managed, except by another professional.

The professional's intellect is invaluable in an IT transformation process. They add intellectual rigour to the decision-making process, looking several moves ahead and interpreting the consequences of decisions. As a leader of change, the professional will be thorough and the vision and plan will be well thought through.

# CHAPTER SUMMARY

The role of the chief technology officer (CTO) is pivotal in navigating the rapid technological changes impacting business strategies.

As technology increasingly defines business success, the CTO's role extends beyond managing technology to integrating it deeply within the broader business goals and leadership activities.

## Build a High-Performance Tech Team

**Strong tech leadership:** ensure senior technology leaders align with organizational, strategic, and technological goals, fostering a cohesive vision.

**Talent management:** focus on attracting, developing, and retaining top tech talent by cultivating an environment that values continuous learning, career growth, and being a great place to work!

**Culture of innovation:** lead initiatives to foster a culture of innovation, where the CTO promotes experimentation and the application of technology to solve complex business challenges.

**Continuous learning:** establish continuous learning programmes to keep the tech team updated with the latest technologies, methodologies, and industry trends, ensuring the organization remains at the forefront of technological innovations.

**Ethical technology use:** the CTO must be involved in setting guidelines for the ethical use of technology, emphasizing integrity and transparency in data usage, and the implementation of AI and other technologies across the company.

# CHAPTER 7

# Developing Great Software

## Changing the Mind of the Organization

*It's all so simple, Anjin-san. Just change your concept of the world.*
*~ James Clavell, Shōgun*

*The ultimate test of agility is whether you can keep all your stakeholders happy.*
*~ Jurgen Appelo*

*Software is a great combination between artistry and engineering.*
*~ Bill Gates*

# On Being Agile

Agile has now proven itself as the best way to develop software. However, if we're embedding software development and operations deeply into the organization, then agile comes as part of the deal. Agile is not "done" by the IT folks; it's "done" by everybody. Let me strengthen that: agile is not about doing; it's about being. It needs to be an enterprise-wide way of doing business.

DevOps augments agile and reinforces its fundamental principle of adding value fast. DevOps is a blend of practices and tools designed to increase an organization's ability to deliver applications and services at high velocity.

There is a natural tension built into the way we run our businesses: shareholders and other stakeholders want as much certainty as possible. They want to know exactly how much revenue and profit is going to be generated in precisely what timeframes. They want quarterly updates on progress towards goals. They want risks identified in forward-looking statements. They want to know whether to buy or sell the company.

At the other end of the scale, product development, sales, and marketing are uncertain endeavours where serendipity can play an important role. It is rarely entirely predictable when a new product will be available and whether the end result will be what the customer wants and is prepared to pay for. The pressure from stakeholders filters through the company to put developers under stress to deliver on time. Stress is a good thing and a bad thing. Too little and we don't feel challenged. Too much can be demotivating and even fatal.

The world would be much easier, complain the developers, if a) the stakeholders would stop applying pressure, b) the people who spec the product could state exactly what they want at the start and not change their minds, and c) the budget (time and money) was sufficient to develop the product. The reality is that a) market pressure is intrinsic and unrelenting, b) people will always change their minds and want maximum flexibility to do so up to the last minute, and c) time and money are always limited.

Agile and DevOps break through the cycle and the paradigm of developers "supplying" a product to a "user" requirement. The agile team (sometimes referred to as a squad, crew, or pod) is a multidisciplinary group of business and technology people working together purposefully to achieve common goals that will add value for the business.

When an agile team is embedded in a business unit, it is sometimes referred to as a BizDevOps team. If we add a security team member, then we get BizSecDevOps. This all gets a little too much alphabet soup for me, so for our discussion here I'll stick with the shorthand DevOps – development and operations – regardless of its constituent parts. The team as a whole does development, and the team as a whole does the operations – including security and business matters. The Ops part is often where the magic happens. Giving a team the freedom and the responsibility for running an application that serves the business and, directly or indirectly, its customers, has an immediate effect on the culture and priorities of the team: everybody is focused on the outcome of adding value. So, operations is not business operations or IT operations. It's both.

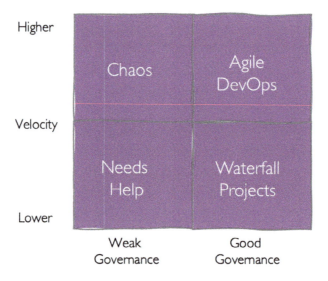

In this chapter, we'll review the agile and DevOps essentials and look at how agile can be further enriched to better handle the transformation and AI priorities in a fusion organization.

# Software Process Automation

Historically, IT folks have been unexceptional at automating their own processes. This has now changed thanks to advanced tooling – especially in a cloud environment.

Automation has become a critical component of successful software development processes. As organizations strive to deliver high-quality software products and services at an ever-increasing speed, the need for automation becomes more pressing. Automation not only enables teams to work more efficiently and effectively but also helps to reduce the risk of human error and ensure consistency across the development life cycle.

One of the key areas where automation is essential is in what is known as continuous integration and continuous delivery (CI/CD). By automating the build, test, and software deployment processes, teams can ensure that code changes are quickly and reliably integrated into the main codebase, tested for quality and functionality, and deployed to production environments. This automation allows for faster feedback loops, enabling teams to catch and fix issues early in the development process, reducing the risk of costly delays and rework down the line.

With the rise of cloud computing and the increasing complexity of modern software architectures, manually provisioning and managing infrastructure has become a daunting task. By using infrastructure as code (IaC) practices, it is possible to write software that defines the virtual infrastructure configurations required to run an application. Defining infrastructure in software terms, as opposed to configuring hardware boxes, makes it extremely flexible, repeatable, and self-documenting.

Automation also helps with compliance and security. By integrating automated security testing and scanning tools into the development process, teams can identify and address potential security issues early on, reducing the risk of data breaches and other security incidents. Additionally, automation can help ensure compliance with industry standards and legislation by enforcing policies and best practices consistently across the organization.

AI-powered testing tools can automatically generate test cases based on the analysis of user behaviour and application usage patterns. Similarly, AI-powered monitoring and alerting systems can detect anomalies and predict potential issues before they impact the end users.

The ultimate AI software development application is the democratizing of computer programming. A significant portion of coding tasks, especially those that are repetitive or based on well-understood coding patterns, can be automated. Tools like GitHub Copilot are already suggesting chunks of code that developers can use, modify, or learn from. Over time, we will see an increase in the percentage of code generated by AI.

However, complex, innovative, and highly customized coding tasks are likely to remain a human-driven endeavour… at least for the foreseeable future. Yet the direction of travel is towards the most popular programming language on Earth being English.

# Agile Plus DevOps for Spectacular Improvements

DevOps aims to shorten the development life cycle of software, while also ensuring the quality and efficiency of the technical operations that support it. In simpler terms, DevOps helps software developers (Dev) and operations teams (Ops) work together more effectively. By breaking down barriers between these two groups, they can quickly build, test, release and deploy software that is reliable and allows the business to respond more rapidly to changing requirements. This cooperative approach not only speeds up the process of getting software to market but also enhances overall product quality and customer satisfaction.

The performance improvement of applying agile and, more importantly, DevOps is spectacular, as evidenced by Forsgren, Humble and Kim in their well-researched book on the science of lean software development:[30]

**Deployment frequency:** high-performing teams deploy code to production much more frequently – possibly many times per day, on demand. Low-performing teams might deploy once per month or with even less frequency.

**Lead time for changes:** high-performing teams have a short lead time, enabling them to move from code "commit" (that is, code completed by a development) to code successfully running in production in less than an hour. Low-performing teams may take between one and six months to push changes to production.

**Change failure rate:** high-performing teams experience a change failure rate of 0–15%, meaning changes are more likely to succeed without causing outages or service impairments. Low-performing teams experience a change failure rate of 46–60%, indicating a higher likelihood of problems with new releases.

**Time to restore service:** high-performing teams can restore service in less than one hour in the event of an incident or outage caused by a change. Low-performing teams might take between one week and one month to recover, significantly impacting service availability and user satisfaction.

These metrics evidence the differences in automation, process efficiency, team collaboration, and organizational culture between high- and low-performing teams. High-performing teams excel due to strong DevOps practices. They employ continuous integration and continuous delivery, automated testing, and proactive monitoring. Their culture supports quick feedback, rapid iteration, and high accountability. In contrast, low-performing teams often face challenges with manual processes and siloed functions. These barriers prevent them from achieving fast and reliable delivery and recovery processes.

# Conway's Law Revisited

Conway's Law suggests that the architecture of a system will reflect the social, political, and power structures of the organization that created it. This principle has profound implications for modern software development and the structuring of organizations, particularly as businesses pivot towards more agile, flexible forms of working.

To build elegant software, we need to align the organizational structure with the desired architecture of the software being developed, or at least mitigate the potential shortcomings of the structure. For instance, a company organized into highly specialized, siloed departments might produce software that is fragmented, reflecting the compartmentalized communication paths within the company. Conversely, a company that promotes cross-functional teams and open communication is more likely to develop integrated, cohesive software systems. This alignment – or misalignment – can significantly impact the efficiency of development processes, the scalability of software, the user experience, and, ultimately, success or failure.

The adoption of agile and DevOps methodologies in software development is a direct response to the challenges highlighted by Conway's Law. These methodologies emphasize collaboration, cross-functional team structures, and continuous feedback loops, aiming to break down organizational silos and encourage more holistic, cohesive system designs. By reconfiguring teams around product or value streams rather than vertical specializations, companies can create systems that are more adaptable and aligned with user needs.

Conway's Law has implications for organizational culture and change management. As businesses embark upon digital transformation, the need for flexible, adaptable system architectures becomes paramount. This often requires a corresponding shift in organizational structures and communication patterns to support the development of such systems.

Conway's Law reminds us that technological change is deeply intertwined with organizational change, and that efforts to innovate in product development must be accompanied by efforts to innovate in organizational design.

# Organization Structures Are Not Built to Last

Organization structures are not built to last – at least not for very long. They are built to reflect the current imperatives. They meet the current requirements of the market, the people, the technologies, the political and social climate, and, not least, the latest fashion trends. As new dimensions are added to organizations, they become increasingly challenging to understand.

Agile was created in the era when software development was the domain of the IT folks. This is no longer the case as "citizen developers" (as Gartner calls them) are increasingly automating their processes with only minimal facilitative support from the technology experts.

Modern organizations are chaotic systems: their future behaviour is never exactly predictable and the 2D organization chart doesn't even come close to representing what is really happening in the real world.

To prevent organizational complexity ending in a quagmire of coordination and bureaucracy, we need to drive not only IT capabilities but also leadership as far into the edges of the organization as we can.

Leadership is a vital ingredient because we need to succeed *in spite* of the organization structure and not ***through*** it. In this world, the requirement for communication skills and creativity is at least as important as the need for analytical thinking – though we still need bags of both!

# Organizational Design – Models and Frameworks

Organization design remains a fundamental instrument in the leadership toolkit. The organization designer has evolved from engineering processes and organization charts to configuring and designing an organizational ecosystem. An ecosystem is inherently fluid and can absorb change. An ecosystem goes beyond the boundaries of an organization and into its customers' and suppliers' ecosystems. Rules in these structures are not always easy to find. Links appear with ease and without planning… often without authority. The ecosystem will adapt and morph into a shape to meet imperatives as they arise.

Agile thinking has evolved rapidly over the last decade and various models, or frameworks, have emerged to help businesses adopt an agile way of working. These models provide structured approaches and best practices that organizations can tailor to their specific needs. When "going agile", it's vital to have a common vocabulary for organizational design, process design and communication. Each model offers unique strengths, and the choice depends on an organization's specific needs and context. Here's a glance at a number of common models:

**Scrum** is a popular agile framework that emphasizes iterative development, collaboration, and adaptability through short, focused work cycles called "sprints".

**SAFe (Scaled Agile Framework)** provides a structured, hierarchical approach to scaling agile practices across large organizations, focusing on alignment and efficiency through agile "release trains" and lean portfolio management.

**LeSS (Large-Scale Scrum)**, on the other hand, extends Scrum principles to large-scale projects, prioritizing simplicity and minimalism by maintaining a single product backlog.

**The Spotify model** promotes team autonomy and alignment with its flexible structure of squads, tribes, chapters, and guilds.

**DAD (Disciplined Agile Delivery)** offers a hybrid framework that integrates agile and lean practices, tailoring processes to project goals.

**Team topologies** (discussed later in the chapter) focuses on optimizing team structure and interactions, categorizing teams into stream-aligned, enabling, complicated subsystems and platform teams.

**The unFIX model**, by Jurgen Appelo, stands out for its emphasis on adaptability and modular organizational design, promoting continuous improvement and dynamic role allocation. This flexibility allows it to integrate various methodologies, making it a versatile meta-framework.

# The Route to Agile

The performance of teams has long been recognized as a critical part of organizational behaviour and success. There's plenty of literature supporting this generally accepted premise and the below references are some personal favourites.

In *The Wisdom of Teams*,[31] Katzenbach and Smith argue that the team should be the basic unit of performance for most companies, irrespective of their size. They show that team performance is far greater than individual performance and that teams form the most common characteristic in successful change in organizations.

In what was arguably the first popular business book, *In Search of Excellence*,[32] Peters and Waterman reported on the "skunk works" they found at a major corporation. The skunk works was a small team of individuals working outside the normal corporate structure to create new products in a hurry. The authors describe the skunk works as a group of between eight to ten people.

In Fred Brooks' legendary (at least in the IT business) collection of essays on software engineering, *The Mythical Man-Month*,[33] he expounds the virtues of the small team as the fundamental building block in software development. Brooks compares the development team to a surgical team comprising different disciplines but all focused on the same goal.

## ING Bank's Transition to Agile DevOps

In *Accelerate*,[34] Forsgren et al discuss ING Bank's extensive implementation of agile and DevOps methodologies, highlighting their shift to value stream-based structures. ING reorganized its teams into "squads", each responsible for a specific value stream, encompassing all necessary roles like developers, operations, and business analysts. This structural change facilitated end-to-end ownership of products, improving collaboration and accountability within the teams.

Each squad at ING follows agile practices, employing iterative development and continuous delivery to ensure rapid and reliable software deployment. These squads are grouped into "tribes", which focus on related areas of functionality, promoting coherence and synergy across the organization. By breaking down silos and encouraging cross-functional teamwork, ING was able to enhance its responsiveness to customer needs and market changes.

The transformation at ING was driven by a strong emphasis on leadership and a culture of continuous improvement. Leadership at ING fostered an environment of trust and empowerment, enabling teams to experiment and innovate without fear of failure. This approach not only improved software delivery performance but also significantly boosted employee engagement and satisfaction, demonstrating the impact of aligning organizational structure with value streams.

The most popular form of agile software development is Scrum. Scrum was developed by Jeff Sutherland and Ken Schwaber.[35] They borrowed the rugby reference from an article written by Hirotaka Takeuchi and Ikujiro Nonaka in the Harvard Business Review.[36] This article compared high-performance teams to the game of rugby. In rugby, the team aspires to move the ball towards the goal line as a unit, passing the ball rapidly among the players. They contrast this approach to traditional relay race development where fixed pieces of work are completed before handing on to the next "runner".

# Agile and Lean

Agile is based heavily on lean manufacturing principles. Lean was exemplified in the fourteen principles of **The Toyota Way**[37] and the work of W. Edwards Deming after the Second World War. In fact, agile borrows unashamedly from the principles first established at Toyota.

As Liker is keen to point out, The Toyota Way increased the dependence on people rather than reducing it. Liker describes it as a system, but also as a cultural approach that allows people to continually improve the way they work. Agile aspires to the same reliance because it puts people at the core.

Both agile and lean have the elimination of waste as a central theme. Waste is any part of a process that does not add value for the customer. Put simply, if the customer is not willing to pay for it, then it is not valuable.

Agile may also be used in any context where today is not (quite) the same as yesterday. For example, in data centres or network operating centres where the systems remain essentially the same from day to day, but the types of issues that arise may vary significantly. Such systems also rarely stay the same for any length of time – new bits are added; software is changed; configurations are changed; traffic patterns change, and so on. A stable state never exists in reality.

# Governance and Rituals (Or Ceremonies)

There is a common misconception that agile is a carefree, easy-going, even undisciplined, way of working. If poorly implemented, it can be. If done well, however, agile is very tightly orchestrated. Certainly, it offers teams the freedom to work together, be creative, and maintain healthy stress levels, but this is achieved within guard rails of structure and method.

The key aspects to agile governance reduce and replace pre-agile committees and processes. Not everybody will use all the aspects in the same way. Some may also prefer a different naming convention, but the idea is generally the same.

The key aspects are arranged in a hierarchy from periodic strategic budgeting to the definition of large chunks of work (called epics), smaller chunks of work (called features and user stories), quarterly business reviews, backlog management (work to be done), to sprint planning and review, to daily stand-up meetings.

## Budgeting and Strategy

This involves setting and managing the financial framework that supports an organization's agile projects. In essence, this is about senior leadership deciding where to place the bets... where to invest money and resources. These decisions will drive the size and number of agile teams to be involved in any particular area of the business.

This process aligns financial resources with strategic business goals, ensuring that investments are targeted towards areas with the highest potential impact. By maintaining a flexible budget that can adapt to feedback and changing market conditions, this governance element ensures resources are optimally allocated to support the right initiatives.

## Definition of Epics

An epic is a large, broad development initiative that represents a significant business goal or set of related goals. An epic is similar to a project, but a project has a much stricter relationship with time, money, resources, and deliverables – it is this overly strict relationship and proneness to costly failure that agile aims to solve.

By breaking down strategic objectives into epics, organizations provide a high-level roadmap for teams to follow, ensuring that each team's efforts contribute directly to larger business outcomes. Regular discussions between executives and agile teams help keep these epics aligned with evolving business strategies.

## Features and User Stories

A feature represents a defined piece of functionality that provides specific value to the user and is governed as part of the broader objectives outlined in an Epic. As a subset of an Epic, a feature is scoped and prioritized to ensure alignment with the overall product vision and goals.

A feature is broken down into user stories, each of which is manageable within a sprint, allowing the team to track progress and deliver incremental value. All code released to production can be directly traced back to a user story, a feature and an epic.

## Quarterly Reviews

Quarterly reviews are scheduled events where multiple agile teams synchronize their development efforts and discuss progress on overall epics. (In the Scaled Agile Framework,[38] these reviews may support the "release train" mechanism.)

The quarterly review ensures that all teams are aligned with the organization's delivery schedule and strategic goals. It allows for managing dependencies between teams effectively and provides a regular forum for adjusting strategies based on the overall performance of the teams and their alignment with business objectives.

The quarterly review can be very effective as a way of getting all the participants (product owners, architects, engineers, etc.) into the same place at the same time. It can become a major cultural reinforcer and great way to engender communication and make friends outside the normal agile and business routine.

## Backlog Refinement

The backlog is a prioritized list of tasks and requirements that agile teams use to organize the work that needs to be done on a project.

Through regular backlog refinement sessions, teams update and prioritize this list to ensure it continues to reflect the most current business priorities, enabling effective sprint planning. This process keeps the backlog relevant and useful, ensuring that teams are focused on the tasks that deliver the most value.

## Sprint Planning and Review

A sprint is a set period during which specific work must be completed and made ready for review. Sprint planning involves defining what can be delivered in the upcoming sprint cycle and setting clear objectives. The subsequent review sessions then assess what has been accomplished during the sprint, providing opportunities for continuous learning and adjustment, which is crucial for maintaining agility and improving project outcomes.

## Daily Stand-Ups

Daily stand-ups (so-called, because they should be short enough that you shouldn't need to sit down) are brief daily meetings used by agile teams to discuss progress, plan day-to-day activities, and address immediate challenges. These meetings help maintain clear communication and quick resolution of issues, ensuring that daily tasks align with the sprint goals. They are essential for keeping the team on track and for executives to gain insights into operational challenges, facilitating swift decision-making to support team productivity.

# People

People are, not surprisingly, the most important element in agile. The premise is that people have a fundamental drive to contribute and want success for themselves and the teams and organizations to which they belong. So agile sets people free to add value, be creative, resourceful, and enjoy what they do. Agile appeals to beyond-the-pay-cheque motivation and provides an environment for autonomy, mastery, and purpose. An agile team is a self-managing unit. For an organization not accustomed to this level of freedom, this can form a major cultural change and needs to be approached accordingly.

**The Product Owner (PO)** is the person who is ultimately responsible for the delivered product. The PO informs the team what features are required and what the priorities for the features are. The PO must be fully empowered to make choices that influence the product. The PO manages the product backlog and ensures that the development team understands the requirements for successful delivery. This role serves as the key liaison between stakeholders and the development team to ensure that the product aligns with business goals and meets user needs effectively.

**The Scrum Master** (in Scrum-based teams, other methods use other nomenclature) serves as the team's facilitator, ensuring that the agile practices are followed and that the team functions smoothly. This role involves removing impediments that may slow down the team's progress, coaching team members on agile principles and ensuring that the team operates in an environment where they can be most productive.

The Scrum Master also facilitates various agile ceremonies, such as daily stand-ups, sprint planning meetings, and retrospectives, to ensure continuous communication and improvement. The Scrum Master may be a full-time role or part-time and executed by any team member. The role may also be rotated amongst the team.

**The development team** builds the product required by the Product Owner with features being developed in priority sequence. The team has a high degree of autonomy to manage its own work rate and chooses how much work can be accomplished in a given period of time.

A team should consist of all the disciplines required to create a working product. However, during execution of a body of work, these disciplines are not strictly adhered to and may not form division-of-labour type lines of work delineation: it is the team that commits to achieving a piece of work, and if a quality assurance engineer (for example) encounters a problem, then the rest of the team should jump in to help out.

The performance of a team increases naturally with time. Over time, people get used to working with each other and know what the team can and cannot achieve. They come to know each other's strengths and weaknesses, support each other, celebrate successes, and learn collectively from failures.

## A Typical Team Shape

A team will typically comprise the following skill sets:

- **Product Owner**.
- **Subject Matter Expert** – for example: on legal, risk, compliance or finance issues.
- **Business Architect (BA)** who understands the business and helps the PO translate business requirements into technology designs for engineers to work with.
- **Design capability:** from crafting the overall customer (journey) experience (CX) to designing the detail of the user interface (UI or UX).
- **Software engineering:** designs, develops, tests, and maintains software applications and systems to meet PO requirements aligned with the BA, UX and UI designs.
- **Platform engineering:** designs, builds, and maintains the (cloud) infrastructure to meet the requirements of the PO and software engineers. This is done using code to create a software-defined infrastructure.
- **Specialists:** data scientist; AI engineer; machine learning engineer.
- **Support:** Scrum Master; agile coach.

This is not an exhaustive list, and not all skills will be required in all teams. Equally, not all the skills may be required all the time. A skill set is not the same as a person: one team member may have multiple skill sets and roles. The more specialized roles may work across several teams. Because team performance naturally improves over time, the team membership should be kept as stable as possible.

# Team Sizes

At the smaller end of the scale, the optimal size for an agile team is widely acknowledged to fall between five and nine members. Renowned psychologist

George Miller, in his seminal paper "The Magical Number Seven, Plus or Minus Two", [39] observed, "There seems to be some limitation built into us either by learning or by the design of our nervous systems."

Miller's observation highlights the cognitive limitations of human beings when it comes to processing information and managing interpersonal relationships within a group setting. With too few members, a team may lack the diversity of perspectives and skill sets necessary for innovation and problem-solving. Conversely, with too many members, communication channels can become congested; decision-making processes can become cumbersome; and individual contributions may be diluted.

In his work *Managing the Human Animal*, Nigel Nicholson provides further insight into our ancestral roots, noting that hunter-gatherer tribes consisted of up to one hundred and fifty individuals, imprinting this as a comfort threshold in our brains. Anthropologist Robin Dunbar found that one hundred and fifty is the magical number for social groups. He discovered a connection between the size of the brain and group sizes by studying primates.

The implications of what is known as "Dunbar's number" extend beyond social relationships to the design of organizational structures and team dynamics. It suggests that there is an upper limit to the size of a cohesive group, beyond which subgroups or specialized teams may be necessary to maintain effective communication and collaboration.

These figures – around seven and around one hundred and fifty – resonate intuitively. They serve as useful benchmarks when designing our teams and groups of teams. For instance, a larger group can be composed of ten to twenty agile teams, allowing for effective collaboration and cohesion.

By breaking down larger entities into smaller, autonomous units, organizations can optimize the benefits of agility while minimizing the inherent complexities associated with large-scale coordination and decision-making.

The concept of team size optimization extends beyond the realm of cognitive constraints to encompass considerations of team dynamics, role clarity, and interpersonal relationships. Within an agile context, the composition of a team should be carefully curated to ensure a balance of skills, personalities, and perspectives.

## Delivering on Time

Agile argues that big projects run late and fail to meet stakeholders' requirements and that the best way to deliver value is incrementally, one step at a time. However, we have a business to run, and meeting (or exceeding) promises is an integral part of being in business. An agile approach cannot therefore be a laissez-faire style of developing product. "It's ready when it's ready" is not an acceptable approach. Self-managed teams can lead to self-managed chaos if the right parameters are not set and monitored.

In business, you need to do what you say you're going to do. In other words, deliver upon commitments. This starts with the strategic plan and cycles through the organization to every team and individual (at least that's the theory). Shareholders expect the CEO to deliver on their plans; for listed companies, this expectation is reflected in the share price.

Agile works in sprints of a couple of weeks and nothing is committed to be delivered beyond the next sprint. Many software developers feel more comfortable and are indeed more productive in situations of low stress.

We therefore have an intrinsic tension between the customer (or stakeholder or shareholder) who wants a guaranteed delivery date with guaranteed functionality, and the developers who are committing to the next two weeks of work. The good news is that this problem can be solved. The hard news is that there is no silver bullet. Adopting an agile style of organization is a question of seeing what works for you and what doesn't. Most organizations go through several iterations lasting some months before arriving at a level that feels like success.

If you're starting from scratch, apply all the rules of Scrum (or another agile approach), master them and understand the underlying principles as well as the mechanics of the implementation. Once mastered, the approach can be adapted to your specific situation.

The beginning may be a little messy, as with all change programmes, and an agile implementation is never a steady state; it is a continuous evolution. The teams will constantly evolve and develop and innovate to improve the way they work. And that is part of the joy of *being agile*!

## The Impact of AI

AI can automate routine tasks and analyse complex datasets more efficiently than humans, potentially reducing the need for large teams for certain domains. However, this shift increases the demand for skills in AI and data science within agile teams. As a result, teams may become smaller but more specialized, requiring professionals who not only understand software development but also how to integrate and work with AI technologies. Seven, plus or minus two may become three, plus AI.

Although data science and AI are distinct fields, their integration into an AI-augmented agile development environment is deeply interconnected. AI systems are trained in data – so poor data quality leads to poorly trained models. Data science lays the groundwork for AI by preparing and analysing data, ensuring that AI models are trained on accurate and insightful datasets.

For software engineers, the integration of AI means an augmentation of their capabilities rather than a replacement. Engineers will need to understand how to work alongside AI, using it for tasks such as code generation, testing, and debugging, while focusing their efforts on more strategic, creative, and complex development tasks where AI can add less value.

In essence, the integration of AI into agile methodologies doesn't just change the technical landscape; it shifts how teams are structured, how they prioritize work, and the nature of the development process itself. Agile teams will need to adapt to these changes, embracing new tools and practices.

# Team Topologies

In designing anything, it helps to have a common design language. So too in designing an organization built of teams. Our ambition in designing any organization is to maximize efficiency whilst being a great place to work; we aim to create a social system that provides a sense of overall purpose, clear responsibilities, autonomy for the teams, and a culture of strong collaboration across the teams.

In their excellent book *Team Topologies*, Matthew Skelton and Manuel Pais[40] offer a highly useable framework for organizing software development teams in a way that optimizes workflow and enhances productivity. The authors identify four primary team types, each with specific responsibilities and characteristics that contribute to the overall agility and efficiency of the organization:

## Stream-Aligned Team

Focused on delivering value directly to customers or users, these teams are aligned around a single, continuous flow of work, often centred on a specific product, service, customer journey or value stream. Their primary goal is to understand and meet customer needs rapidly and efficiently, requiring a deep understanding of the business domain and a close alignment with customer objectives.

These teams need to be very tightly aligned with the business. They typically report to a business or product owner or a business lead who has a clear understanding of customer requirements and strategic business objectives.

In terms of employee headcount, stream-aligned teams usually account for the bulk of the IT-related payroll budget.

If outsourcing part of the product development or service delivery, the external team could be treated as a stream-aligned team, focusing on delivering value directly to users or customers. Clear goals, regular communication, and alignment on user needs are crucial.

## Enabling Team

These teams provide specialized capabilities and knowledge that other teams need to do their work but might lack the skills or resources to develop internally. Enabling teams help by sharing expertise, tools, and practices, often working temporarily with other teams to overcome specific challenges or to foster new capabilities.

Enabling teams will provide services that any single stream-aligned team may not need on a permanent basis. For example: agile coaching, architecture support, security testing, UX design, compliance guidance, or some specific technology – perhaps AI!

They would typically report into the CTO or head of engineering, especially in technology-focused organizations.

Outsourcing of enabling teams may be beneficial for organizations seeking to enhance their capabilities or fill gaps in expertise without expanding their internal headcount permanently.

## Complicated Subsystem Team

When certain parts of the system are highly complex or require deep technical expertise, a CST may be required. Such systems might be, for example, a machine learning model or a specialized data storage system. The software they develop would typically be used by a stream-aligned team to create some kind of service. CSTs might report to the CTO or engineering lead for tech-related cases.

Outsourcing highly specialized or technical work fits naturally with the complicated subsystem team concept. These external teams can handle specific, complex parts of the system that require deep expertise, functioning independently but aligned with the organization's technical standards and architecture. However, if the subsystem is mission-critical for the firm, outsourcing may not be the ideal long-term strategy.

## Platform Team

Serving as the foundation for other teams' work, platform teams develop and maintain the set of tools, services, and infrastructure that enable other teams to deliver value more efficiently. The platform is treated as an internal product, with the platform team actively seeking to understand and address the needs of their "customers" (i.e. the other teams within the organization).

In a modern cloud setting, the platform team would typically be responsible for cloud management, tool selection, security, and platform cost management. They would provide a suite of services (infrastructure as code) to the stream teams to allow them to deploy and maintain their own infrastructure systems. This enables the stream teams to operate at a high level of autonomy and delivery velocity.

By providing a standardized service, the platform team contributes to overall governance, security, and compliance of the IT function.

The platform team may be outsourced, but this is handle-with-care outsourcing. As these teams serve many other teams, they are mission-critical and must perform well — from an architectural and a detailed technology implementation perspective. The choice of outsourcing partner is therefore critical. A hybrid model is not unusual here whereby specific areas are outsourced to a specialist supplier while others are retained in-house.

Platform teams would typically report to the CTO.

# CHAPTER SUMMARY

Agile and DevOps have revolutionized software development by emphasizing collaboration, flexibility, and continuous improvement, enabling organizations to deliver high-quality products and services more efficiently.

To reap the full benefits from agile and DevOps, organizations must embrace a culture of innovation, breaking down silos and empowering teams to work autonomously within a framework of clear guidelines and responsibilities.

## Massively Boost Productivity with Agile and DevOps

**Talent acquisition and retention:** success in any technology strategy hinges on hiring and retaining the right talent. High HR engagement is crucial for transitioning to and embedding agile and DevOps practices across the organization.

**Agile and DevOps culture:** foster a culture where all departments, not just IT, adopt agile and DevOps practices, ensuring a holistic approach to (technology) innovation and efficiency.

**Cross-functional teams:** create multidisciplinary teams that blend business and technology expertise, working collaboratively to achieve shared goals.

**Automation priority:** invest in automation tools for testing, deployment, and monitoring to minimize errors, streamline processes, and reduce manual workload.

**Continuous improvement:** encourage regular feedback and continuous improvement by establishing feedback loops and retrospectives, enabling the organization to adapt and improve processes continuously.

# CHAPTER 8

# Continuous Product Innovation

## Boundless Opportunity and a Strong Moral Compass

*Make your requirements less dumb. Your requirements are definitely dumb… doesn't matter who gave them to you. Everyone's wrong some of the time. Requirements come with a name, not a department.*
*~ Elon Musk*

*The role of the product organization is to consistently deliver significant new value to the business through continuous product innovation.*
*~ Marty Cagan*

# Lessons from The Valley

To embark upon any innovative product initiative is to see the future as something we can create, not as something coming towards us to which we must react. No place on Earth does that better than The Valley.

Silicon Valley has been the greatest innovation engine in the world for the last few decades. Silicon Valley is not an organization; it is not orchestrated or managed. In fact, it is an incredibly chaotic sprawling mass. Silicon Valley is a network of people. There is no bureaucratic or political hierarchy. If you have one of the raw materials The Valley needs, such as money, talent, or an idea, then you are welcomed into the unofficial club.

Silicon Valley is an ecosystem for innovation centred on Stanford University. Members of the ecosystem include high-tech businesses, entrepreneurs, leaders, lawyers, coaches, engineers, designers, and, of course, the providers of the oil of the innovation engine, the people with the money. The intricacies of The Valley's social networks are as complex as the nanometre communication paths etched into the chips that gave it its name.

The lessons from Silicon Valley are not to get in the way of innovation, not to stifle it with bureaucracy, to build strong networks, both inside and outside your organization, and to have a little fun along the way.

## Iterative Development and the AI Impact

Taking their cue from Silicon Valley, product organizations must embrace the agile and iterative approach that emphasizes rapid experimentation, continuous learning, and the ability to pivot quickly in response to changing market conditions.

The key to success in this new paradigm is to build products incrementally, using validated learning to guide decisions and prioritize features based on real customer feedback. Validated learning[41] is the process of testing hypotheses and measuring the results to gain a deeper understanding of what works and what doesn't. It involves collecting data on how customers interact with a product, analysing that data to identify patterns and insights, and using those insights to inform future product decisions. By releasing products early and often and using data to measure their impact and identify areas for improvement, organizations can reduce waste, mitigate risk, and ensure that they are delivering value to their customers. Ultimately, this approach requires a fundamental shift in mindset, from one that values certainty and predictability to one that embraces uncertainty and sees failure as an opportunity to learn and improve.

Traditionally, the PO role (I use the term PO but it may be a CPO, head of product, product manager or any other title with product responsibility) has focused on balancing customer needs, technology capabilities, time pressures, and budgetary constraints. The PO leads a team to blend technology with design to solve customer problems and add value to the business.[42] POs must now also have an understanding of how they can integrate AI into their products.

The scope of product ownership now extends beyond traditional tech boundaries to include a deeper understanding of AI's technical and ethical dimensions. The integration of data-driven decision-making tools, the necessity for ethical guidelines in AI deployment, and the strategies for enhancing customer experiences through personalized approaches can all be added to the PO's (already considerable) skill set.

# Applying AI

AI's ability to process large amounts of data and recognize patterns enables POs to offer more personalized and efficient user experiences. Whether it's improving customer retention, enhancing service interactions, or ensuring product quality, AI opens up new possibilities for innovation.

The possibilities are endless, but to offer a flavour of what's going on, I'll explore five specific ways AI is currently enhancing products across different industries, illustrating its potential to create significant business efficiencies and competitive advantages.

## Intelligent Customer Service Chatbots

AI-powered chatbots can transform customer service by providing fast, 24/7 support to users. These chatbots use natural language processing (NLP) to interpret customer requests accurately and machine learning to improve responses over time.

One of the most immediately impacting and well-documented[43] use cases for AI is from payment services company Klarna. In its first month of operation, the AI chatbot processed two-thirds of all Klarna's support requests – some 2.3 million conversations – with a satisfaction score equivalent to human agents. It took over the work of seven hundred agents. Resolution reduced from eleven minutes to two minutes. Overall, enquiries dropped by 25% due to the accuracy of the initial resolution. It's available 24/7 in thirty-five languages. Estimated bottom line impact for the year: $40 million.

## AI-Enhanced Quality Control

In sectors like manufacturing, AI can significantly enhance product quality and consistency. A PO overseeing a manufacturing line might implement AI systems equipped with computer vision to inspect and analyse the quality of products in real time during the manufacturing process. These systems can detect defects or deviations from the standard that are imperceptible to the human eye.

Tesla employs sophisticated AI-driven systems across its production lines.[44] These AI systems are integrated into their manufacturing processes to analyse data from various sensors and cameras, detecting potential defects or deviations from standard specifications in real time.

## Predictive Analytics for Customer Retention

AI plays a crucial role in enhancing a product's ability to retain customers by directly analysing vast amounts of user behaviour data and making accurate predictions about potential churn. By applying machine learning algorithms, AI systems can process and interpret complex patterns within user data, enabling businesses to identify at-risk customers with a high degree of precision.

US telco company Sprint uses predictive analytics models to identify customers who are at risk of churning and then takes proactive steps to retain them.[45] By analysing data points such as call quality, customer service interactions, billing information, and usage patterns, Sprint's models can predict which customers are likely to leave in the near future. Armed with this information, Sprint reaches out to these customers with targeted offers, discounts, or service improvements to address their specific issues and improve their overall satisfaction, effectively reducing churn rates.

### Automated Personalization Engines

AI enables dynamic personalization at scale, which is particularly beneficial in e-commerce. A PO can utilize AI to tailor the shopping experience for each visitor in real time. For example, AI algorithms analyse past purchases, browsing history, and search queries to dynamically adjust the displayed products, deals, and advertisements to fit the user's preferences. This level of personalization can lead to increased sales and customer satisfaction as users experience a more intuitive shopping environment that seems uniquely curated for their needs.

Amazon uses AI-powered recommendation engines to suggest products to users based on their browsing and purchase history, as well as the behaviour of similar users. They also apply AI and machine learning models to recommend a size that's "just for you" on each product's detail page.[46]

### Sentiment Analysis and User Feedback Processing

AI can help product owners gain valuable insights from user feedback and sentiment analysis. By using NLP and machine learning techniques, AI algorithms can automatically analyse user reviews, social media mentions, and support tickets to identify common issues, sentiment trends, and feature requests. This enables product owners to make data-driven decisions, prioritize product improvements, and address user concerns more effectively.

X (Twitter) uses NLP sentiment analysis[47] to understand the emotions and opinions expressed in the vast amount of user-generated content on its platform. By analysing tweets in real time, X can gauge public sentiment around various topics, trends, and events. This information is valuable not only for X itself but also for businesses, governments, researchers, and public figures who want to monitor their brand reputation, track customer feedback, or understand public opinion on specific issues.

# Ethics and Bias

Ethical considerations and governance are crucial as AI technologies become more embedded in products. With great power comes great responsibility, and POs face this challenge head on. They must ensure AI is used responsibly in their products.

POs need to protect data privacy. As they collect and use more consumer data, it's vital to keep this information safe and private. They must follow laws and regulations to protect user data from misuse or breaches.

Bias in AI models is a serious concern. AI systems learn from data. If the data is biased, the AI's decisions will reflect these biases. POs must work to identify and correct these biases to ensure fairness. They need to test AI systems thoroughly and keep refining them to avoid discriminatory outcomes.

Making ethical decisions is a constant requirement. POs must consider the wider impacts of their choices in AI integration. This means thinking about how the product affects its users and society at large. Ethical product development involves more than following rules. It requires a commitment to positive values and the welfare of others.

# Portfolio: Big Bets and Small Bets

AI and digital transformation have a core aim to be innovative and to help us reimagine the way we do business. This requires a rethink of how we balance our product portfolios across R&D, business as usual and big, corporate bets. With AI, cloud, and other new technologies (at least, new for an organization), small bets and innovative R&D projects are useful for getting used to the experience and starting to get the flywheel spinning. In the early days, you'll need a few champions of the new tech: talented evangelists who are empowered to take risks.

Innovative solutions or new products can be created in major strategic initiatives but are often found in smaller-scale projects, or (often) by accident. A corporate strategy will typically comprise a mix of big bets and small bets. Small bets are usually off-the-wall ideas, pilots, and projects. A big bet is a major decision that is not easily changed and has a fundamental impact on the future. A big bet may be a choice to go in one direction and not another. It may also be a decision not to do something, or to discontinue a particular product line or area of business.

A small bet is an entrepreneurial initiative, an adventure, an experiment.

Small bets are not unimportant, but they're not catastrophic in the event of failure. Big bets are always strategic in impact. Small bets will be part of the strategy but will also arise on a daily basis as ideas, innovations, and initiatives. At any one point in time, there will be a portfolio of initiatives, big bets and small bets.

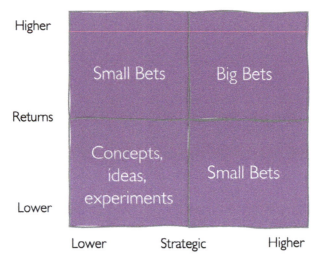

Bets can migrate up the portfolio from ideas and initiatives to strategically significant programmes or to tactical high-return projects. Further migration can be made into the big-bet quadrant for ideas that can transform the way the company operates. We've seen this with the two most valuable companies in the world (as I write this): NVIDIA (erstwhile maker of PC graphics cards for games) and Microsoft (who supplied IBM with an operating system for their first PC). Entrepreneurship isn't always a question of founding a company on a great vision; it can often be a question of recognizing an opportunity when it comes across your path.

# Transformation and the Customer Experience (CX)

Customer experience (CX) has emerged as a cornerstone of effective digital transformation strategies. CX encompasses every interaction a customer has with a brand, spanning the entire journey from initial awareness through to post-purchase support and beyond. Successful digital transformation applies CX to foster deeper, more meaningful relationships with customers.

Digital transformation is not only about technology and processes; it's about people and how they interact with digital services.

CX encompasses all interactions between a customer and a company, from the initial awareness stage to post-purchase support. It's not just about the product or service itself, but the overall satisfaction a customer feels throughout their journey. CX is about emotion – the perception of using a product or service.

CX can get confused with user experience (UX), but there's a distinct difference between the two. UX focuses on the usability and functionality of a specific product or service, such as a website or mobile app. It's about designing an interface that is intuitive, efficient, and enjoyable to use. CX, on the other hand, takes a holistic view of the entire customer journey, considering every touchpoint and interaction across multiple channels.

To create a truly exceptional CX, organizations need to bring together two key roles: enterprise architect and CX designer – they must make a great team! Enterprise architects are responsible for ensuring that the organization's technology is aligned with its business goals and can support the desired customer experience. They take a strategic view of the organization's systems, processes, and data, and work to create a cohesive and scalable architecture.

CX designers are focused on understanding the customer's needs, preferences, and behaviours. They use a variety of methodologies, such as:

- **User research:** conducting interviews, surveys, and observations to gain insights into customer needs and pain points.
- **Persona development:** creating fictional characters that illustrate different customer segments, based on their demographics, behaviours, and goals.
- **Customer journey mapping:** visualizing the steps a customer takes to complete a task or achieve a goal, identifying opportunities for improvement along the way.
- **Prototyping and testing:** creating low-fidelity or high-fidelity prototypes of new features or services and testing them with real users to gather feedback and iterate on the design.

By working together, enterprise architects and CX designers can create systems that both meet the needs of the customer and provide architectural integrity. This means ensuring that the technology used is flexible, scalable, and secure, while also delivering a seamless and personalized experience across all touchpoints: products that are a joy to use.

# CHAPTER SUMMARY

The chapter underscores the strategic and evolving role of product owners and the need for them to develop a deeper understanding of AI's technical capabilities and associated ethical dimensions.

POs must now embrace AI to create new, exciting, and valuable products while also ensuring responsible use.

## Drive Innovation with AI and Data-Driven Strategies

**Culture of experimentation:** encourage teams to embrace uncertainty, take calculated risks, and view failures as growth opportunities. Shift the mindset from seeking certainty to quickly adapting based on validated insights.

**Invest in AI and data:** equip POs and their teams with the necessary tools, resources, and training to effectively apply AI and machine learning.

**Customer-centric AI:** use AI to deeply understand customer needs, preferences, and behaviours. Utilize this data to create more personalized and efficient customer experiences.

**Ethical AI governance:** establish ethical guidelines and governance structures for responsible AI use, addressing data privacy, bias detection, and broader societal implications. Ensure POs and their teams understand the ethical dimensions.

**Collaborative culture:** foster cross-functional collaboration and knowledge sharing among POs, AI experts, and other stakeholders. Promote regular retrospectives and iterations based on customer feedback and market insights.

# CHAPTER 9

# Architecting the Enterprise

## Bringing Order and Elegance to Business and IT

*Everything we do at the agency is for people; no matter what the project is, it is for people. It is so that people can get the most out of a building.*
*~ Giorgio Bianchi, Architect RPBW[48]*

*The task of an architect is to bring order and relation into human surroundings.*
*~ Dr Steen Rasmussen, Experiencing Architecture[49]*

*Small is beautiful.*
*~ E.F. Schumacher[50]*

# Elegance

At the core of Renzo Piano's design for The Shard (the tallest building in London) lies the concept of lightness and transparency. Despite its towering stature, The Shard was envisioned to be an elegant spire, setting it apart from the bulkier high-rises of earlier times. Great architecture goes beyond being functionally useful and aesthetically pleasing; it moves us emotionally; we feel a sense of *wow!*

The modern business architect (I'll distinguish the various types of business architecture in a minute) faces similar challenges to Renzo Piano's Shard: to create inspirational blueprints, bringing disparate parts of an organization and its systems together to create elegance, lightness, and transparency, and thereby crafting a baseline for agility, speed, and flexibility whilst meeting regulatory and compliance requirements. That's a long sentence… I'll try to unpack it in the rest of this chapter.

A business architect must make things simpler, clearer, more understandable – revealing and defining the links within and across an organization. A part of this process is challenging the requirements in the same sense that a PO must do, but at a more fundamental level. The architect asks the challenging (and not infrequently annoying) strategic questions about why, who, when, how, and what.

A building architect's work is essentially finished when the building is in place. In business, the architect's job continues long after the initial design and build phases, continually shaping and adapting to a changing world whilst keeping the foundations secure to ensure the integrity of the structure above. An organization is never a static entity; it is fluid, moving, dynamic, changing, responding constantly to its environment. A business architect doesn't so much design a steady state structure as create an organic ecosystem where all the parts interact with each other. An organization interacts with other organizations outside its own boundaries, thereby linking itself to other ecosystems. Shaping the totality of such a complex endeavour is what makes architecture so fascinating, challenging, and rewarding.

An enterprise architect produces deliverables such as strategic roadmaps, architectural blueprints, and technology standards. These artifacts include detailed diagrams, reference models, and documentation that ensure technology solutions align with business goals and integrate seamlessly across the enterprise.

The Shard is elegant by design. A well-crafted business architecture is also likely to be elegant – it makes sense; its design is clear; the connections to business strategy and structure are well defined; it's efficient and meets budgetary and other constraints. If it's inelegant, it's less likely to inspire those who must use it and may even not be fit for purpose.

## From "Enterprise" to "Chief" Architect

Dutch global bank Rabobank designates the top EA role as Chief Architect, highlighting its significance within the organization. Recognizing IT and architecture as crucial, the bank's supervisory board appointed a chief innovation and technology officer (CITO) to the management board.

At the time of writing in the magazine *IT Executive*,[59] the CITO had nine direct reports: the chief architect, chief data officer, chief information security officer, four chief technology officers, and the heads of strategy and innovation and agile transformation.

The CTOs cover retail banking, wholesale and rural, risk and finance, and engineering and employee sectors.

The bank scrapped the CIO title in 2017.

# Enterprise Architecture – Creating Order and Relation

The concept of enterprise architecture has evolved significantly since its introduction in the 1980s. Initially focused on addressing the growing complexity of IT systems, enterprise architecture has now expanded to encompass a wide range of components, including strategy, business processes, data, applications, and technology infrastructure. This broad approach is essential in fusion organizations, where the boundaries between business and IT are blurred.

## The Role of EA in Fusion Organizations

The shift towards fusion organizations is driven by the need to use technology as a strategic enabler, rather than a mere support function. In fusion organizations, IT is no longer a siloed department but an integral part of every business unit, driving innovation, efficiency, and customer value.

In this distributed agile/DevOps context, the role of enterprise architecture becomes even more critical. Architecture provides the glue that holds the various components of a fusion organization together. By establishing a shared vision and a set of guiding principles, the EA helps to align the efforts of diverse teams and stakeholders, reducing duplication and improving collaboration.

EAs must work closely with business leaders and domain experts to drive technology strategy and innovation across the organization. Some organizations have taken this relationship a step further and have placed EAs as joint heads of business with a business unit manager. This fundamentally changes the EA role from being a strategic advisor to having "skin in the game" and being accountable for the business results.

## Enterprise Architecture as a Driver of Digital Transformation

Digital transformation isn't just about adopting new technologies; it's about fundamentally rethinking the way organizations operate and deliver value to customers. In this context, enterprise architecture plays a critical role in driving the transformation agenda. By providing a complete view of an organization's current state and future goals, the EA helps to identify opportunities for innovation and optimization.

One of the key challenges of digital transformation is the need to balance the competing demands of agility and stability. On the one hand, organizations need to be able to quickly adapt to changing market conditions and customer needs. On the other hand, they need to ensure that their core systems and processes remain reliable and secure. The EA helps to strike this balance by providing a framework for managing change in a controlled and predictable manner.

An important aspect of digital transformation is the need to leverage data as a strategic asset. With AI, organizations that can effectively capture, manage, and analyse data will have a significant competitive advantage. The EA plays a key role in this regard by establishing a data architecture that ensures data quality, security, and accessibility. By providing a clear set of standards and guidelines for data management, the EA enables organizations to harness the power of data and drive better decision-making.

## Challenges and Considerations

While the benefits of enterprise architecture are clear, implementing an effective EA programme is not without its challenges. One of the most intricate is the need to secure buy-in from stakeholders across the organization. EA initiatives often involve significant changes to existing processes and systems, which can be met with resistance from those who are comfortable with the status quo. To overcome this resistance, EA leaders need to communicate clearly, but also have the political "clout" to get things done.

Another challenge is the need to balance the desire for standardization with the need for flexibility. While establishing a clear set of standards and guidelines is essential for ensuring consistency and interoperability, it's also important to allow for some degree of local variation to accommodate the unique needs of different business units and teams. Enterprise architects need to strike the right balance between control and autonomy, providing a framework that is both uniform and adaptable.

Despite these challenges, the benefits of enterprise architecture for digital transformation and AI are too significant to ignore. As the pace of technological change continues to accelerate, the role of the EA will only become more critical in ensuring that organizations can thrive… and avoid plunging into chaos if at all possible.

# Data, Application, and Infrastructure Architecture

In addition to the key role of the enterprise architect, who focuses on the overarching IT strategy and alignment with business goals, there are other specialized types of architects essential in the technology landscape. The data architect is responsible for designing and managing the organization's data architecture. The application architect oversees the design and development of software applications, ensuring they meet business requirements and integrate seamlessly with other systems. And the infrastructure architect focuses on the physical and virtual (cloud) infrastructure.

Nomenclature may differ from one organization to another, and there is no holy grail for how best to organize architecture functions in business. My definitions here are based loosely on the industry standard TOGAF model,[51] but there are other frameworks that provide blueprints for how the discipline may be structured and executed. Smaller organizations may have all the roles in a single person, whereas larger firms will have dedicated staff operating across the business.

## Data Architecture

Data architecture outlines the organization's management and storage of logical and physical data assets. The output of this process includes data models, data dictionaries, and database schemas that facilitate effective data governance and ensure data is accessible, reliable, and secure across the enterprise.

A data architect may report into a business line or into a specialist supporting function under the CTO.

## Application Architecture

Application architecture provides a blueprint for the deployment, interaction, and relationship of applications to the organization's business processes. The outputs from this architecture include application specifications, integration requirements, and an interaction diagram that delineates how each application connects and shares information, ensuring alignment with business strategies and goals.

Application architects may report into the business line in a fusion organization. However, a reporting line into IT (the CTO) is also a well-trodden path.

## Infrastructure Architecture

Infrastructure architecture defines the software and hardware capabilities required to support the deployment of business, data, and application services.

Its outputs are detailed specifications of the IT infrastructure, including network diagrams, hardware specifications, software needs, and standards for communications and data processing. This ensures the technology stack (as it is called) is joined up, scalable, secure, and capable of supporting current and future business requirements.

The infrastructure architect will typically report into the tech side of the business under the CTO.

# Technology Challenges for Architects

As with any new technology or business change, EAs need to ensure that AI and agile/DevOps are integrated into the overall IT strategy. This includes selecting appropriate AI tools and platforms that support organizational goals. In most cases, this will involve selecting a cloud service provider and one or more AI platforms to ensure that the infrastructure can scale as needed.

AI workloads can be computationally intensive and require significant processing power and storage capacity. This requires architectures that can scale horizontally and vertically to accommodate the demands of AI systems.

AI and fusion structures pose specific challenges for the EA:

- Data quality for input to AI models (LLMs and other).
- Loosely coupled architectures to facilitate agile/DevOps teams using APIs to communicate between systems.
- Governance and ethics.

We'll explore each of these in more detail.

## Data Quality Challenges

AI relies heavily on vast amounts of data to train models and generate insights. If you are relying on an AI (or any other system) to make decisions for you or advise you, then getting the data right is the starting point.

Ensuring data quality is paramount in AI and machine learning; the old adage "garbage in, garbage out" is still very applicable. In a typical corporate environment, data can become outdated or out of sync for several reasons, and architects and data scientists must employ specific strategies to address these issues.

There are a number of ways in which data can become less useful, or even damaging, for application in AI systems:

- **Data decay:** over time, data can become obsolete or irrelevant.
- **Siloed data:** in many organizations, data is stored in disparate systems or departments, leading to inconsistencies and synchronization issues.
- **Manual data entry errors:** human error during data entry can lead to inaccuracies.
- **Lack of data governance:** without good data governance policies, there can be inconsistencies in data formats, standards, and usage, leading to data quality issues.
- **Rapid changes in business environment:** in fast-paced industries, data can quickly become outdated due to rapid changes in the market, technology, or regulatory environment.

## Strategies to Ensure Data Quality

Architects must focus on designing data-centric architectures that can support the collection, storage, processing, and analysis of massive volumes of structured and unstructured data. This requires a deep understanding of data management, data governance, and data quality principles, as well as knowledge of big data technologies and platforms.

Architects must work closely with data scientists and AI experts to design structures that can handle the complex data flows and processing requirements of AI applications. They need to ensure that AI systems are designed with transparency and ethical considerations in mind, to mitigate potential risks and biases.

A number of approaches can be employed to improve the data quality of existing systems:

- **Data cleaning:** regularly clean data to identify and correct errors, such as duplicates, inaccuracies, and inconsistencies.
- **Data integration:** implement data integration solutions to ensure data from different sources is consistent and synchronized.
- **Data governance:** establish data governance frameworks that define data standards, quality metrics, and usage policies.

- **Automated monitoring and alerts:** use automated systems to monitor data quality continuously.
- **Regular audits and updates:** conduct regular data audits to assess quality and relevance.

With the ethical and legal considerations around AI, a governance structure to ensure compliance and security is a concern to be addressed not only by the EA but by the organization as a whole.

## Agility and Loosely Coupled Architecture

"Small is beautiful", as Schumacher famously formulated it in his bestselling book[52], which carried the (appropriate for our discussion here) subtitle: "A Study of Economics as if People Mattered".

Architects are typically champions of agile methodologies and design principles that prioritize speed and agility over rigid, monolithic architectures. This includes the adoption of microservice architectures, containerization (comparable to shipping containers but for software), and DevOps practices that enable teams to develop, test, and deploy new services quickly and independently.

A loosely coupled architecture envisions a system that is not a monolithic whole, but a federation of small components whereby each one has a clear delineation of responsibility. Each component has defined inputs and outputs that allow it to communicate with other components – most likely through APIs or through a messaging system. This architecture is a crucial prerequisite for a DevOps implementation where teams have a high degree of autonomy. In other words, the loosely coupled tech design supports the loosely coupled organization design.

A single component must be capable of being released to production without having a negative impact on any other component. As components are small, they are more easily tested and can be released rapidly, thereby reducing time to market for any changes. This means that components need to be versioned so that other components can "talk" to a previous version if they need to. Typical properties of loose coupling are:

- **Encapsulation:** each component in a loosely coupled system encapsulates its own data and behaviour, hiding the internal details from other components. This encapsulation reduces dependencies and minimizes the impact of changes in one component on others.

- **Communication through contracts:** loosely coupled components interact with each other through well-defined contracts or interfaces, such as APIs or message queues. These contracts specify the input and output of each component, allowing them to communicate and collaborate without needing to know the internal details of one another.
- **Technology independence:** loose coupling promotes technology independence by allowing components to be developed using different programming languages, frameworks, or platforms, as long as they adhere to the defined contracts and interfaces.
- **Scalability and resilience:** loosely coupled systems are easier to scale horizontally (for performance) by adding more instances of individual components as needed. They also tend to be more resilient to failures, as the failure of one component is less likely to bring down the entire system.
- **Evolutionary design:** loose coupling supports evolutionary system design, enabling organizations to adapt and extend their systems incrementally over time by adding, modifying, or replacing individual components without requiring an extensive rework of the entire system.

OK… that might sound a little technical, so here's an example: let's consider an e-commerce platform that sells products to customers worldwide. The platform consists of several microservices, each responsible for a specific function, and these microservices are loosely coupled to ensure flexibility, scalability, and maintainability. Each microservice may be developed by a discrete agile team.

The e-commerce platform includes microservices such as product catalogue service, inventory service, order management service, payment, shipping service, and customer service. Each microservice is developed and deployed independently, perhaps using different technologies and programming languages best suited for their specific tasks. They communicate with each other through well-defined APIs, such as RESTful endpoints or message queues, without needing to know the internal details of one another.

The user interface (UI) of the e-commerce platform is designed as a separate microservice, responsible for presenting product information, managing user interactions, and coordinating with other microservices to provide a seamless user experience (UX). The UI microservice communicates with the product catalogue service to display product details, images, and pricing information. It also interacts with the customer service microservice to handle user authentication, account management, and personalized recommendations.

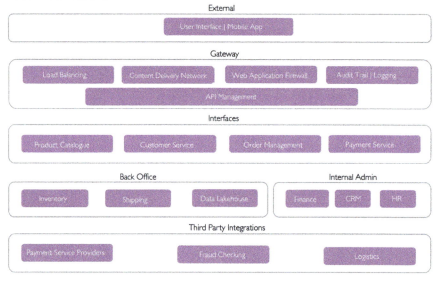

Example of a basic application landscape for e-commerce

If the customer decides to purchase a product, the UI microservice or mobile app communicates with the order management service to create an order. The order management service then validates the order by checking the product availability with the inventory service and sends a payment request to the payment service. Once the payment is processed successfully, the order management service updates the order status and sends a shipping request to the shipping service.

Throughout the purchasing process, the UI service keeps the customer informed about the order status and provides a smooth and intuitive user experience. Using loose coupling and microservice architecture, the e-commerce platform can easily update and enhance the UI without affecting the underlying services, ensuring a flexible and adaptable user interface that can evolve with changing customer needs and preferences.

## Governance

Architects need to establish appropriate governance frameworks that can effectively manage the complexity and risks associated with AI and ensure that technology decisions are aligned with business objectives. This requires a shift from traditional, centralized governance models to more agile and distributed approaches that can keep pace with the speed and scale of digital transformation.

Architects must therefore work closely with business leaders, data scientists, CX designers and AI experts to develop governance policies and processes that promote transparency, accountability, and ethical use of AI. This includes establishing clear roles and responsibilities, defining decision-making processes, and implementing monitoring and control mechanisms to ensure that AI systems are performing as intended and delivering value to the organization.

Architects should ensure that governance frameworks are flexible enough to accommodate the rapidly evolving nature of AI technologies and can adapt to changing business needs and regulatory requirements. Establishing effective governance can help mitigate risks, drive innovation, and ensure that technology investments are optimized to deliver real value to the enterprise.

# CHAPTER SUMMARY

Enterprise architecture plays a critical role in driving digital transformation and AI adoption. It provides a framework for aligning IT with business goals and organizational structures, thereby reducing the negative side of Conway's Law.

In fusion organizations, where IT is deeply embedded across the entire enterprise, enterprise architecture becomes central to establishing a shared vision, fostering collaboration, and driving innovation.

## Empower Enterprise Architecture for Transformation

**A comprehensive approach:** embrace an enterprise architecture strategy that integrates business processes, data, applications, and technology infrastructure to ensure IT and business alignment.

**Digital transformation driver:** utilize enterprise architecture to spearhead digital transformation by identifying innovation opportunities and getting the ball rolling.

**Data architecture:** develop a data architecture that aims to guarantee data quality, security, and accessibility, enabling better decision-making.

**Agile design principles:** adopt agile design principles like loosely coupled architectures and DevOps practices to enhance speed, agility, and flexibility in developing and deploying new services.

**Effective governance frameworks:** implement governance frameworks that ensure transparency, accountability, and ethical AI use, while remaining flexible as AI evolves.

# CHAPTER 10

# Cybersecurity Threats and Opportunities

## Embrace Security by Design and Don't Hit the Headlines

*Is it safe?*
*~ Sir Laurence Olivier's Dr Szell in the film* Marathon Man

*An ounce of prevention is worth a pound of cure.*
*~ Benjamin Franklin*

*Trust arrives by foot and departs by horse.*
*~ Dutch proverb*

# What is it?

Cybersecurity is a large and complex field that remains relatively new, so let's start with a definition: cybersecurity is the strategic, risk-based application of processes, technologies, and people-centric measures to safeguard IT assets from digital attacks and accidental damage. This chapter's mission is to unpack and make sense of this definition in an AI/digital context without getting lost in jargon.

Into an already challenging security landscape, we are now adding new technologies, new organization structures, and artificial intelligence. And we're doing it all as fast as we possibly can. Changing so many variables at high speed is risky and potentially chaotic.

Introducing DevOps or any of the technologies discussed in this book will increase the attack surface of an organization. For example, AI tends to reduce the cost of complexity – and if the price of something decreases, then we tend to get more of it. AI capabilities can also be opaque in their reasoning, and a lack of explainability causes problems not only for security but also for compliance. If your AI cannot explain how it arrived at a particular conclusion or decision, how can you tell it hasn't been hacked or maliciously trained on incorrect data?

To raise the position of cybersecurity even higher on boards' agendas, regulators are issuing billions in fines[53] for breaches, and senior executives are being held personally liable[54] for security or regulatory mistakes – ignorance is not a defence.

How should we address cybersecurity in the age of AI, remote working, decentralized team structures, complex digital ecosystems, and internet-based client interactions? Applying more top-down controls, rules, and frameworks challenges the very foundations of agile and DevOps. Adding to the growing mountain of sophisticated tooling increases complexity, and gaps may appear between the tools. Increasing overall cybersecurity budgets is hard to sustain, and even harder to defend – how much is enough? How much is too much?

We must find solutions with new technologies to replace the old approaches, but also with a people-centric approach.

This chapter aims to serve as an introduction to the subject matter and looks at the opportunities available to keep our systems safe so we can be trustworthy participants in the marketplace.

## Trust

We prefer to do business with people and organizations we trust – it's an innately human trait. Trustworthiness is fundamental and not something you can claim to be; it is something that must be earned over time.

### The Estonia Story[55, 56]

In 2007, Estonia faced major cyberattacks that lasted for weeks, disrupting key services across the country. These attacks overwhelmed the online services of Estonian banks, media outlets, and government bodies with unprecedented levels of internet traffic.

Estonia has now transformed itself into a global leader in digital security through its innovative digital identity system. Every citizen has a digital ID that grants secure access to a wide range of online services, from voting to banking.

This system is protected by advanced encryption, ensuring that all digital transactions are private and secure. Estonia's commitment to cutting-edge technology ensures that sensitive information is shielded from cyber threats.

At the core of Estonia's digital security is blockchain technology, which guarantees the integrity and transparency of transactions. This tamper-proof system maintains trust and reliability, making it nearly impossible for data to be altered or corrupted.

Estonia's approach demonstrates the power of combining advanced encryption and blockchain to create a trust framework. This model provides a practical blueprint for other nations and organizations aiming to enhance their digital security and protect against cyber threats.

In a digital business context, trust means having confidence that information shared is properly protected and that the integrity of transactions is maintained.

Reliable cybersecurity measures reinforce this trust: when an organization demonstrates a strong commitment to cybersecurity, it not only protects its own assets but also reassures its partners and customers that they are a trustworthy participant.

Geopolitical turmoil and full-blown warfare have underlined how quickly the risk landscape can change for any organization or country.[57] Cybersecurity breaches shake our trust in the systems that keep our economies and societies running, while other technology-based risks, such as disinformation, can be equally destabilizing. The threat from nation-state actors for commercial organizations is a "real and present danger" as the World Economic Forum phrases it, and such attacks are indeed well documented.[58]

Both public and private organizations are re-examining the vulnerabilities in their systems and processes, from customer service to democratic elections. Of major concern is how disinformation, deepfakes, and sophisticated phishing campaigns can, and are, being weaponized to disrupt our institutions and businesses. While information warfare isn't new, the spread of IoT, AI and other tech developments have put defending against these types of threats at the top of the priority list.

# Cybersecurity and Compliance

Cybersecurity is easily conflated with compliance. While there are areas where they intersect, they are fundamentally different – being compliant doesn't necessarily mean being secure, and vice versa. While compliance involves adhering to specific standards and regulations, cybersecurity requires a proactive approach to protect against a broad spectrum of evolving threats, beyond fulfilling legal or regulatory obligations.

Compliance requirements start with defining the scope. For example, the Payment Card Industry Data Security Standard (PCI DSS) is a comprehensive security baseline designed for payment processing, specifically focusing on the flow of credit card data through an organization. However, this standard does not encompass other systems, such as a CRM system: an organization might be fully PCI DSS compliant yet still have vulnerabilities, such as an unnoticed back door into the customer system.

This may be a contentious proposition, but if you have to make a choice between security and compliance, choose security. Sometimes it's better to ask for forgiveness rather than permission.

# Cybersecurity and Business Continuity

Business continuity and cybersecurity are two domains that, while distinct, significantly overlap in ensuring the resilience and operational stability of an organization. Both fields aim to protect the organization's assets and operations, albeit from slightly different perspectives. Both business continuity and cybersecurity aim to minimize disruptions. Business continuity focuses on maintaining essential business functions during and after an incident (any incident – not cyber per se), while cybersecurity aims to prevent, detect, and respond to cyber threats that could cause disruptions.

For our discussion here, I'm taking the angle of cybersecurity, but the methods and solutions also provide a significant slice of a business continuity strategy. As an example, an online transaction processing system may be architected across multiple (cloud) data centres with a high level of application resilience against component failure. This might be aimed at ensuring that the application is highly available for customers with a low mean time to repair (MTTR). This is fundamentally a business choice and an application architecture question, not a cybersecurity one. However, the cybersecurity approach for the application must be fully aligned to ensure it supports the business objective. In other words, the application protects against component failure (software, hardware, database etc), whereas cybersecurity protects against a cyber threat such as a distributed denial of service (DDoS) attack.

Underlying both business continuity and cybersecurity is an understanding of the assets that a company has, what these assets do, how important they are, and who the owner of the asset is. The owner is a person (or role) who is empowered to make decisions about the asset. For products, this will be the Product Owner. For infrastructure, it may be a head of systems engineering or a similar role.

The use of the so-called CIA matrix – Confidentiality, Integrity, and Availability – provides a useful (and commonly used) framework for evaluating the importance of an asset.

- **Confidentiality:** protecting sensitive information from unauthorized access.
- **Integrity:** ensuring the accuracy and reliability of data.
- **Availability:** guaranteeing that information and resources are accessible when needed.

Each asset in the organization is allocated a score across the three dimensions. This can be used for IT assets but also non-IT assets. The specific scoring method will vary depending on the organization, but a common approach involves using a numerical scale (say, three, two, one) or high/medium/low rating. For example, an online transaction processing system would typically score high on all three ratings, whereas an internal HR system may have a high confidentiality and high data integrity but a lower acceptable availability.

If your organization doesn't have a good asset list and CIA rating yet, this is worth doing. The result may be a simple spreadsheet list or a fully populated database (there are many good asset management SaaS solutions available). The process and the discussions to arrive at the ratings are a useful way of involving all disciplines across the business in the decision-making process.

# Who Is Accountable?

Executing a resilient cybersecurity strategy is not the sole responsibility of the CISO; it requires a concerted effort across the entire organization. Ensuring that all stakeholders understand and commit to cybersecurity measures is crucial for the strategy to be effective and for the organization to be resilient against cyber threats. While the CISO is responsible for strategy development, monitoring, and auditing, the execution of the strategy must be a shared responsibility involving the CEO, CTO, and other senior leaders.

Noteworthy here is that the EU NIS2 directive (effective from October 2024) introduces significant changes to cybersecurity regulations within the EU, particularly emphasizing accountability at the executive level. It specifies that senior management and executives can be held personally accountable for non-compliance with cybersecurity risk management requirements. Being breached can be a career-limiting experience.

The CEO plays a critical role in establishing a cybersecurity-centric culture within the organization. By prioritizing cybersecurity at the executive level and integrating it into the overall business strategy, the CEO ensures that all departments recognize the importance of strong security measures. This top-down approach helps in fostering a security-aware culture, where employees at all levels understand their role in maintaining the organization's cybersecurity posture.

The CTO is instrumental in aligning the technical infrastructure with the cybersecurity strategy. This involves ensuring that the organization's technology stack is secure, implementing advanced security measures, and staying abreast of emerging threats and technologies. The CTO collaborates closely with the CISO to ensure that security protocols are not only implemented but also regularly updated and tested. Indeed, in smaller organizations, the CISO may report into the CTO, or they may be the same individual.

## The 2024 CrowdStrike Incident[59]

On July 19, a faulty configuration update to CrowdStrike's falcon sensor software caused massive disruptions for organizations using Microsoft Windows.

The update triggered a memory error that led to widespread system crashes, affecting around 8.5 million devices globally, primarily in corporate environments. Although the issue was resolved within a few hours, recovery for affected businesses required manual intervention, leading to extended downtime for many.

This incident had far-reaching implications, causing operational disruptions in sectors such as air travel, with thousands of flights cancelled. The financial fallout was significant, with estimates suggesting that top U.S. companies collectively faced billions in losses.

# Roles in the CISO Team

A number of tasks need to be completed by the CISO team; whether these tasks are all done by one person or by a large team will be driven by the organizational context. The CISO team would typically require the following skill sets:

- **Governance and policy experts:** develop and enforce security policies, procedures, and standards to align with organizational goals and regulatory requirements.
- **Security analysts:** monitor and analyse security incidents, conduct vulnerability assessments, and respond to threats.
- **Security engineers:** responsible for implementing and maintaining security infrastructure, such as firewalls, intrusion detection systems, and encryption protocols.
- **Compliance officers:** ensure the organization adheres to regulatory requirements and industry standards, managing audits and policy enforcement. May also report into the CRO.
- **Incident response team:** handles the identification, investigation, and mitigation of security breaches or incidents.
- **Security architects:** design and oversee the implementation of secure systems and networks, ensuring resilient defence mechanisms are in place.

## Common Cybersecurity Terminology

**IT assets:** all hardware, software, networks, data, and other components essential to a functioning IT environment.

**Cyber threat:** the possibility of a malicious attempt to breach an organization's security.

**Cyberattack:** a deliberate attempt by an individual or a group to breach the cybersecurity of an organization with the intent to cause damage. Cyberattacks may arrive across the internet, but they may also be from inside an organization.

**Attack surface:** the sum total of all entry points (mostly internet and API connections) and vulnerabilities within an organization.

**Threat intelligence:** the process of collecting, analysing, and utilizing information about current and potential cyber threats.

**Cyber resilience:** the ability of an organization to continue to do business and to bounce back following a cybersecurity incident.

**Security operations centre (SOC):** a centralized unit within an organization that continuously monitors, detects, and responds to cybersecurity incidents to protect against threats.

**Damage** to assets may result in various forms of loss, from reputational damage to financial loss, customer attrition, ransom payments, data theft, legal liabilities, and more.

# Strategic Dilemmas

Developing a cybersecurity strategy is challenging due to the ever-changing cyber threat landscape, the significant costs involved, and the nature of the returns on any investment.

The strategy development process is further challenged by a potential communication gap between chief information security officers and their peers. This is not unusual in the technology space, which tends to be somewhat jargon-laden. CISOs often speak in technical terms such, as those defined above, while non-tech execs are more attuned to business-oriented language and outcomes. This disconnect can make it difficult to convey the importance and impact of cybersecurity investments effectively.

## Ever-Changing Threat Landscape

The cybersecurity threat landscape is poised to become even more challenging, demanding heightened vigilance from business leaders. As digital transformation accelerates, cybercriminals will develop more sophisticated methods of attack, targeting both critical infrastructure and corporate assets with increased frequency and severity. In this evolving environment, we must adopt a proactive approach, using advanced threat intelligence and risk management frameworks to safeguard our organizations.

## RoI and Budgeting

The return on investment in cybersecurity is often nebulous. In many areas of business, the benefits of investments can be directly measured; for example, the net present value (NPV) of future earnings, revenue increase, market share, or net promoter score (NPS). The success of cybersecurity efforts is frequently reflected in an absence – nothing happens. No hacks, no leaks, no ransomware, no incidents. Curiously, the result of investing too much in cybersecurity is impossible to prove. Whereas the results of investing too little may be that the business is hacked and ransomed with potentially existential results. So somewhere along the continuum between total devastation and total overkill lies the Goldilocks zone of investing just enough. A CISO would caution to err on the side of overspending.

How much you spend on security is a question of what industry you're in. As a very general guideline, cyber budgets tend to be around 10% of the IT budget.[60] For certain sectors, such as finance, this can be as high as 15% of the IT budget or almost 1% of company revenue.[61]

# Risk-Based Cybersecurity

Given that it isn't possible to protect all assets all the time from all potential threats, choices have to be made. A risk-based approach to cybersecurity is essential for creating a security strategy that is understandable for both technical and non-technical stakeholders. By focusing on identifying, assessing, and prioritizing risks based on their potential impact, this approach allows organizations to allocate investments more effectively and address the most significant risks first.

In practice, a risk-based approach involves conducting risk assessments to identify vulnerabilities and potential threats. By quantifying the potential impact and likelihood of these risks, cybersecurity teams can present a clearer case for investment to business leaders. This approach translates technical jargon into business language, emphasizing how specific risks could affect the organization's financial health, reputation, and operational continuity.

A heat map offers a further aid to the understanding and prioritization of risks using a matrix grid structure. This visual tool helps to flag areas of risk by plotting the potential impact and likelihood of various threats. Each risk is placed within the grid, providing a clear visual representation of its severity and priority. It's not going to be an absolute truth, but it is a useful aid for discussion and decision-making. The colours (rainbow or greyscale), the size of the matrix and division into categories can be done manually, using an automated tool or AI-generated.

Clearly, you don't really want anything in the critical zone. Identifying a risk is the first step. For example, item 1 in the exhibit might be staff unwittingly sharing sensitive company data with an online AI system outside the company's control. Having identified a risk, the second step is to either accept it, or take mitigation measures to reduce the probability and/or the impact. The action plan, or direction of travel, can also be shown in the grid: for example, from critical to high within four weeks, and from high to medium within eight weeks.

| Impact | | | | |
|---|---|---|---|
| High ③ | High | Critical | Critical |
| Medium | High | High ② | Critical ① |
| Low | Medium | Medium | High ④ |
| Low | Low | Low ⑤ | Medium |

Probability

Example of a heat map with five risks plotted

# Software Development, Shift-Left and Toll Gates

Integrating good cybersecurity practices is fundamental to building resilient application software and infrastructure. Security is not something that can be bolted on at a later stage, and it is extremely expensive to fix at scale – say, after a piece of software has been rolled out to millions of users.

What is required is a mechanism for embedding security as an integral part of the development process. This is often referred to as a "shift-left" strategy – process flows tend to be drawn from left to right, and we want to move security to the left.

Shift-left emphasizes proactive security practices such as code reviews, static analysis, and automated testing. These practices ensure that security is a fundamental part of the development process, rather than an afterthought. For instance, static code analysis tools can automatically scan code for common vulnerabilities, enabling developers to fix issues before they progress further down the development pipeline.

Toll gates are predefined checkpoints in a shift-left strategy whereby specific criteria must be met before a software release can proceed to the next phase. Toll gates act as quality control measures, ensuring that each stage of development adheres to established security standards. For example, a

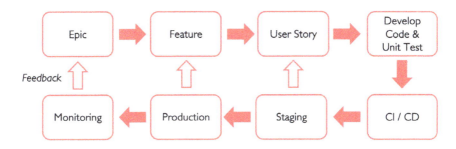

The software development process – phase progress requires that toll gates are met

toll gate might require successful completion of security testing, a four-eyes code review sign-off, a product owner sign-off, or compliance with industry regulations, before moving from development to testing or from testing to production deployment.

Implementing toll gates ensures that security considerations are consistently applied and verified at critical junctures in the development life cycle. This structured approach prevents the accumulation of unaddressed vulnerabilities and ensures that security is integrated into every phase of the software development life cycle (SDLC).

# Legislation, Controls, Frameworks and Certifications

Adopting a cybersecurity framework offers advantages for implementing effective security measures. Such frameworks provide a structured approach to risk management, ensuring all aspects of cybersecurity are systematically addressed. This helps organizations identify and prioritize vulnerabilities.

Compliance with regulatory requirements becomes more straightforward with recognized frameworks. Certification and regular audits build trust with partners, demonstrating the organization's commitment to stringent security practices.

Navigating the world of cybersecurity can seem complex, but understanding the key frameworks and standards can help streamline the approach. To effectively implement cybersecurity, it's often better to focus on one or two standards. For many organizations, starting with widely recognized frameworks like ISO 27001 or NIST (see below) provides a solid foundation.

## Meta's Woes

In November 2022, Meta[66] (Facebook's parent company) was fined €265 million by Ireland's Data Protection Commission (DPC) for a data leak that exposed the personal information of over five hundred million users. This fine was part of a broader investigation into Meta's compliance with the EU's General Data Protection Regulation (GDPR). The breach, initially discovered in 2019, involved the scraping of user profiles using a vulnerability in Facebook's contact importer tool.

The DPC's ruling highlighted Meta's failure to implement appropriate technical and organizational measures to protect user data. This incident underscores the critical importance of data protection strategies and compliance with GDPR requirements to avoid significant financial and reputational damage.

Separately, in 2023, the European Data Protection Board (EDPB) imposed a €1.2 billion fine on Facebook[67] for violations related to data transfers between the EU and the US, marking the largest GDPR-related fine to date. This decision underscores the importance of data protection measures for international data transfers.

If your organization has specific industry requirements, such as finance or healthcare, then clearly these must be adhered to. For example, if your company handles credit card transactions, complying with PCI DSS is essential. Additionally, ensure adherence to regional legislative requirements like NIS2, DORA and GDPR if operating within the EU to cover compliance and data protection laws.

In the sections below, I'll summarize the most common major international standards, legislative controls and certifications used in the industry. This is not intended as an exhaustive list.

## International Standards and Frameworks

- **The ISO 27000 series,** particularly ISO/IEC 27001, offers a global standard for managing information security, focusing on protecting data confidentiality, integrity, and availability.

- **The Center for Internet Security (CIS) Controls** offers practical, prioritized actions to enhance cybersecurity, widely adopted for improving security posture.
- **COBIT,** developed by ISACA, provides a complete framework for IT governance and management, ensuring IT strategies align with business objectives.
- **The Capability Maturity Model Integration (CMMI)** focuses on performance improvement across various domains, providing a structured approach for enhancing quality and efficiency.

## Legislative Controls

Governance bodies across the world are implementing stricter requirements for security, privacy and business continuity. These are considerable pieces of legislation and can be challenging projects, even for the most advanced students. I've included some of the more significant regulations below, but this is by no means exhaustive.

- **The NIS2 (Network and Information Systems) Directive,** implemented by the European Union, mandates stringent cybersecurity measures across various sectors within the EU, emphasizing risk management, incident reporting, and enhanced cooperation between member states.
- **GDPR (General Data Protection Regulation)** is a critical EU regulation, focusing on data protection and privacy, requiring organizations to safeguard personal data and respect privacy rights.
- **DORA (Digital Operational Resilience Act)** is an EU regulation for financial entities. It mandates comprehensive ICT risk management, incident reporting, operational resilience testing, and third-party risk management.
- **The EU AI Act** is a landmark regulation that establishes a comprehensive legal framework for the development, deployment, and use of artificial intelligence, focusing on risk-based regulation to ensure AI is safe, transparent, and respects fundamental rights.
- **The NIST guidelines** in the United States provide a framework for risk management and continuous monitoring, widely used by

both federal agencies and private organizations to enhance their cybersecurity posture.

- **The CCPA (California Consumer Privacy Act)** grants California residents greater control over their personal data.
- **HIPAA (Health Insurance Portability and Accountability Act)** in the US focuses on the security and privacy of health data.

## Certifications

Certifications play a vital role in equipping professionals with the skills needed to implement cybersecurity frameworks. The CISSP (Certified Information Systems Security Professional) from the International Information System Security Certification Consortium (ISC2) covers a broad spectrum of information security concepts.

ISACA offers specialized certifications such as CISA (Certified Information Systems Auditor), CISM (Certified Information Security Manager), and CRISC (Certified in Risk and Information Systems Control).

Finding qualified cybersecurity professionals is exceptionally challenging due to a significant talent shortage in the field, with many organizations struggling to fill critical roles that require certifications. These certifications denote a high level of expertise and knowledge and are highly sought after, making the recruitment of certified professionals a competitive and difficult task.

# The AI Arms Race

AI in cybersecurity is a double-edged sword. While it significantly enhances defensive measures by providing advanced tools for threat detection and response, it also equips cybercriminals with sophisticated capabilities to conduct more effective and damaging attacks. By staying ahead of AI-driven threats, organizations can maximize the defensive benefits of AI while mitigating its potential misuse by cybercriminals.

A recent CISO report by Splunk (a security firm owned by Cisco)[62] found that the vast majority of CISOs (70%) believe that "generative AI will create an asymmetrical battlefield that will inevitably be tipped in favour of cyber adversaries". However, 35% of CISOs are already using AI for security applications, and that number is increasing.

## Offensive AI Capabilities

AI systems don't get tired — they are persistent, can change themselves dynamically without human intervention, can imitate humans almost flawlessly, can learn from failures, can integrate social media and any other internet sources, can process massive amounts of data in real time and can hide on the dark side of the internet. To compound the situation, there are bad actors, such as state-sponsored criminal organizations, with very deep pockets.

As examples for our discussion here, I'll take two types of commonly used attack vectors that can "benefit" from AI: malware and phishing. These AI-generated attacks are becoming increasingly common as they are able to bypass many traditional security measures.

## Malware

AI-driven malware represents a significant challenge for cybersecurity defences. By using advanced machine learning, AI can create sophisticated malware that adapts and learns from previous attacks. This ability allows it to analyse security patterns, modifying its behaviour to bypass antivirus software and intrusion detection systems.

AI malware can also employ "polymorphic" and "metamorphic" techniques, changing its code structure or rewriting itself entirely with each infection. This constant evolution makes it difficult for signature-based detection systems to identify the malware, as it always appears as a new, unique threat. Additionally, AI can target specific vulnerabilities more effectively by using detailed data analysis to identify and exploit weaknesses in software or network configurations.

## Phishing

AI also enhances phishing attempts, making them more realistic and harder to defend against. Using advanced NLP, AI can craft highly personalized messages that mimic legitimate communications, drawing from analyses of social media profiles and email correspondence. This sophistication can deceive even the most cautious users.

AI bots can persistently send phishing emails, adapting tactics based on user responses and exploiting any discovered vulnerabilities with precision.

Combining AI with social engineering techniques compounds the threat. AI can exploit human psychology traits, such as trust and urgency, to manipulate targets into revealing sensitive information. This blend of realism, persistence, and psychological manipulation makes AI-driven phishing a formidable challenge in cybersecurity.

## Defensive AI Capabilities

But it's not all doom and gloom: from a defensive perspective, AI's ability to monitor and analyse vast amounts of data in real time enhances proactive threat detection. Deloitte Insights[63] notes that cyber AI can be a "force multiplier", enabling organizations to not only respond faster than attackers, but also to anticipate these moves and react to them in advance. The use of AI to analyse patterns and predict potential threats before they manifest is a significant leap forward in cybersecurity.

On any IT platform, millions or billions of events occur every day. For example, login attempts, emails, file accesses, network traffic and application events. It's important to note that not all of these events are necessarily security-related or indicative of a threat. The vast majority will be generated by normal user and system activities. DevOps teams will typically build monitoring into their systems and create dashboards to gain insights into how the system is behaving – such as the number of transactions being processed, volume of traffic that is being handled, current response times, number of users logged in and so on. Cloud providers will also provide a mass of data and metrics regarding the behaviour of applications such as memory usage, disc usage, potential security issues. All this monitoring can also generate events to be monitored by security analytics systems.

The volume and type of events can vary significantly based on factors such as the time of day, day of the week, a Black Friday or marketing promotion and so on. There may be more login events during business hours or more network traffic during peak usage periods. Anything unusual that breaks with an established pattern may be regarded as an anomaly.

Cyber defence systems automatically collect and aggregate vast amounts of event data from various sources. By utilizing machine learning algorithms, these systems can analyse the data to detect patterns and irregularities. Rule-based correlations further enhance this analysis, pinpointing potential security incidents or anomalies that might otherwise go unnoticed. When such anomalies are identified, they are flagged for further investigation by the security team. By prioritizing and filtering events based on their risk level and relevance, these tools help security teams focus their efforts on the most critical issues and respond more quickly to potential threats.

# A People-Centric Approach

Nine out of ten data breaches are caused by human error,[64] and if humans don't feel comfortable (or do feel punished) when they make a mistake, then they will be unlikely to report it.

Culture endorses "the way we do things around here", and a positive security culture is a cornerstone of good security. In a fusion organization, a high degree of autonomy for DevOps teams (indeed for all teams) is encouraged — within the guard rails of company policies, architectural, and security guidelines, and... the company culture. A positive cybersecurity culture must be part of the overall organizational culture. The tone at the top is essential in achieving this.

Culture can encourage accountability and agility by providing guidelines for behaviour that are neither explicit nor codified. However, an underregulated or overregulated culture can obstruct change, hinder development and slow growth. If people feel that security gets in the way of them doing their job, they will work around it.

Culture can make people feel comfortable or uncomfortable with their own and with other people's behaviour. Culture makes people feel uncomfortable when they do something that is not aligned with the organization's values as this produces a sense of cognitive dissonance. This may be self-inflicted or triggered by the environment. In other words, people will feel uncomfortable with counter-cultural behaviour either because their culture conscience says that they should, or because other members of their group point out that their behaviour is inappropriate.

Security must be a completely business-as-usual topic. All members of the organization should feel comfortable raising security issues. In the famous Toyota Production System, workers could halt the production line to ensure that an issue was addressed immediately, thereby preventing defective products from moving further down the line. This system was a key aspect of Toyota's approach to quality control and continuous improvement, embodying the principles of "jidoka" (automation with a human touch) and "kaizen" (continuous improvement).

Jidoka and kaizen are equally applicable and valuable in a security context.

## A Just Culture

The idea of a "just culture" originated in the aviation industry and has been used in various high-risk industries, such as healthcare and nuclear power. A just culture is the opposite of a blame culture.

A just culture, in terms of cybersecurity, refers to an organizational mindset that emphasizes accountability and learning from mistakes without resorting to punitive measures. It is a concept rooted in systems thinking, which recognizes that errors and security breaches are often the result of systemic issues within the organization rather than solely the fault of individual employees.

In a just culture, the focus is on understanding and addressing the root causes of incidents to improve overall security practices. When a security breach or mistake occurs, the organization asks, "What went wrong?" as opposed to, "Who is to blame?" This approach encourages employees to report errors, near misses, and potential vulnerabilities without fear of retribution. The goal is to create an environment where continuous improvement is prioritized, and learning from mistakes is a key component of the security strategy.

By fostering open communication and transparency, a just culture helps identify weaknesses in security practices and processes. This proactive stance enables organizations to implement effective solutions that mitigate risks and prevent future incidents.

# CHAPTER SUMMARY

Cybersecurity is the strategic, risk-based application of processes, technologies, and people-centric measures to safeguard IT assets from digital attacks and accidental damage. In the age of AI and digital transformation, organizations face new challenges in maintaining trust, compliance, and business continuity.

Cybersecurity is not solely the responsibility of the CISO; it requires a concerted effort across the entire organization, with the CEO and CTO playing critical roles in establishing a positive security culture and aligning technical infrastructure with the cybersecurity strategy.

## Enhance Cybersecurity in the Organization

**Asset inventory and CIA ratings:** conduct a thorough asset inventory and assign confidentiality, integrity, and availability (CIA) ratings to each asset to prioritize security efforts effectively.

**Risk-based cybersecurity strategy:** develop a cybersecurity strategy highlighting the potential impact of risks on financial health, reputation, and operational continuity.

**Shift-left strategy in development:** implement a "shift-left" approach with toll gates in the software development life cycle to integrate security practices from the early stages of development.

**Adopt cybersecurity frameworks:** embrace recognized cybersecurity frameworks like ISO 27001 or NIST and ensure compliance with industry-specific regulations and regional legislative requirements.

**Foster a security culture:** promote a security culture that encourages open communication, transparency, and continuous improvement, focusing on learning from mistakes rather than assigning blame.

# CHAPTER 11

# Leadership
# and People

## All Change for the Digital Generation

*Human beings generally have a low level of tolerance for uncertainty.*
*~ Manfred Kets de Vries*

*All who have meditated on the art of governing mankind have been convinced that the*
*fate of empires depends on the education of the youth.*
*~ Aristotle*

*When people are financially invested, they want a return. When people are emotionally*
*invested, they want to contribute.*
*~ Simon Sinek*

*Happiness depends on ourselves.*
*~ Aristotle*

# Leadership in the Age of AI

AI and other technologies explored in this book will enable us to make smarter, better informed, and more rational decisions. But will this improved ability make our enterprises more successful?

*Star Trek's* Mr Spock is the perfect rational economic being (most of the time). Human beings are not. Although we can put on a pretty good show of rationality, we are often illogical, unreasonable, neurotic, emotional, anxious, and highly irrational. As *Homo sapiens,* we are more *Homo emotus* than *Homo economicus*.

A good IQ is, of course, not a guarantee for success, and leaders must also have a strong emotional quotient (EQ). Leaders must be bright, but also self-aware and socially-aware, and through awareness be capable of managing themselves and others better.[65] Leadership is demanding and stressful and good physical health (PQ) is required to survive the breakneck pace of change. Yet, in an AI-driven world, another dimension becomes crucial: spiritual awareness, or SQ.

SQ is the ultimate capacity that humans have over and above AI. SQ taps into a deeper sense of purpose, of consciousness, of empowering greater satisfaction in work and life. It's about connectedness, contribution, appreciation, creativity, freedom, love and personal growth. It means recognising our own roles and the roles of our organizations in a more holistic, connected, environmental and human context. SQ provides a template for our behaviour and our beliefs; it provides us with our values and a moral compass.

In times of rapid change, SQ becomes an essential asset by allowing us to intuitively grasp the bigger picture, seeing connections and patterns that logic alone might miss. This intuitive capacity is at the core of SQ, guiding us beyond the boundaries of traditional cognitive thinking. In many ways, intuition is the purest expression of SQ – it's the inner knowing that helps us navigate uncertainty, make decisions with deeper wisdom, and align our actions with a greater purpose.

For leaders, learning to trust intuition is as critical as developing emotional intelligence. While EQ allows us to manage relationships and emotions, SQ sharpens our ability to sense the unspoken, interpret symbols, and foresee risks that aren't immediately obvious through data or rational analysis. When leaders tap into their intuitive intelligence, they are better equipped to adapt to disruptive changes, innovate in unforeseen ways, and foster environments where creativity thrives.

Trusting our intuition is more important now than ever in an AI-driven world where data reigns supreme. While AI can process massive amounts of information, it lacks the human capacity for insight and foresight that comes from SQ. Leaders who cultivate and rely on their intuition can make quicker, more holistic decisions, balancing facts with their inner sense of what's right. This ability doesn't just contribute to personal success; it also ensures long-term organizational success. It directly influences breakthrough innovation, talent retention, and wiser, more thoughtful decision-making – key elements that drive both growth and a healthier bottom line.

What happens when you're in a meeting and your AI team member disagrees with a critical decision you're taking? Ask your intuition.

# Strategic Leadership Roles

The strategic roles essential for leading (the transition to) a fusion organization outlined in this book are Enterprise Architect, Customer Experience Designer, Chief Information Security Officer, and Chief Technology Officer.

The enterprise architect ensures that technology aligns with business goals while promoting innovation and efficiency. The customer experience designer focuses on enhancing user interactions with products and services, driving satisfaction and loyalty. The chief information security officer safeguards the company against cyber threats and helps build a resilient organization. The chief technology officer oversees technological development and strategy, ensuring the organization adopts the best technologies to support the business.

The EA, CTO and CISO are candidates for retention at board or senior executive level.

# The Impact of AI on Job Displacement

While AI and digital transformation offer significant opportunities for growth and innovation, they also raise concerns about job displacement. As machines become increasingly capable of performing tasks previously done by humans, some roles may become redundant. This is not only true for jobs that involve routine, repetitive, or easily automated tasks, but also for creative industries such as film, advertising, writing, and music. However, it is important to recognize that AI is also creating new job opportunities, particularly in areas such as data science, cybersecurity, machine learning, and AI development.

To mitigate the impact of job displacement, organizations must develop effective retraining and redeployment strategies. This involves identifying the skills and competencies that will be most valuable in the digital age and providing employees with the necessary training and support to transition into new roles. Redeployment strategies may include moving employees into different departments or functions where their skills are in high demand or creating entirely new roles that utilize the capabilities of both humans and machines.

# The Importance of Lifelong Learning

The concept of lifelong learning has become more important than ever. The skills and knowledge required to succeed in the workplace are constantly evolving, and employees must be prepared to continuously update and expand their skill sets. Organizations should foster a culture of continuous learning, providing employees with access to training and development opportunities throughout their careers. This may include online courses, workshops, mentoring programmes, and opportunities for experiential learning.

Employees must learn to work alongside AI systems. This requires a new set of skills, including the ability to interpret and analyse data, communicate effectively with both humans and machines, and adapt to new technologies and ways of working.

# Preparing the Next Generation for the Future of Work

We need to prepare the next generation for the challenges and opportunities ahead. This requires a fundamental shift in education and training, with a greater emphasis on digital literacy, problem-solving, and adaptability. For some educational institutions who are still stuck in (almost Victorian) classical learning models and a one-size-fits-all approach, this will require a major overhaul.

Schools and universities must work closely with industry partners to develop curricula that align with the needs of the digital age, providing students with the skills and knowledge required to succeed in the workforce of the future.

Governments and policymakers also have a critical role to play in preparing society for the impact of AI and digital transformation on the workforce. This may include investing in education and training programmes, providing support for workers displaced by automation, and developing policies that promote the responsible and ethical use of AI in the workplace. By working together, governments, organizations, and individuals can help ensure that the benefits of AI and digital transformation are widely shared and that no one is left behind in the transition to the digital age.

# AI in HR

AI offers significant practical HR benefits, but it also comes with the risk of inadvertently creating a "Big Brother" culture if not carefully managed. AI tools can improve efficiency in areas like recruitment by automating the screening of resumes, tracking employee performance, and predicting turnover. However, if not used thoughtfully, these tools may go too far, leading to concerns about surveillance and loss of privacy. The ethical use of AI in HR is critical to maintaining fairness, transparency, and trust within an organization.

HR teams must ensure that systems are designed to be free from discrimination, particularly in areas like hiring where unconscious bias can easily be amplified. This requires regular audits of AI systems to ensure they comply with ethical standards and are aligned with diversity, inclusion and regulatory goals.

Employees should be made aware of when and how AI is being used in HR processes, and human oversight should remain central in decision-making to prevent dehumanization and ensure nuanced judgements and diligence where needed.

# CHAPTER SUMMARY

The rapid development of AI and digital transformation is revolutionizing the workplace, redefining traditional job roles, and creating new positions that require a combination of technical and soft skills.

Organizations must invest in training and development programmes to upskill and reskill their workforce, while also developing effective retraining and redeployment strategies to mitigate the impact of job displacement.

## Seizing the Opportunities… with Care

**Strategic hires:** ensure key positions such as Enterprise Architect, Customer Experience Designer, Chief Information Security Officer, and Chief Technology Officer are filled with strategic hires.

**Skill development:** identify critical skills and competencies for the digital age and provide staff at all levels with the necessary training and support to acquire them.

**Culture of continuous learning:** foster a culture of continuous learning by offering employees access to various training and development opportunities throughout their careers.

**Retraining and redeployment:** develop effective retraining and redeployment strategies to mitigate the impact of job displacement caused by AI and automation.

**Ensure ethical use of AI:** HR must ensure that AI is used ethically and transparently, balancing the need for efficiency with privacy and fairness, while maintaining human oversight in decision-making processes to build trust.

# CHAPTER 12

# What's Next?

Go Boldly

*It is not the strongest of the species that survive, nor the most intelligent, but the one most responsive to change.*
*~ Charles Darwin*

*The only way to make sense out of change is to plunge into it, move with it, and join the dance.*
*~ Alan Watts*

*What's next?*
*~ President Jed Bartlet, played by Martin Sheen in The West Wing*

*The only difference between being a child reading an adventure book and being an adult in the 21st century is that the child can put the book down.*
*~ Will Murray*

# Revisiting Conway's Law Once More

Digital transformation and AI adoption are about fundamentally changing how our organizations operate, communicate, and deliver value. Fusion organizations embody this change by integrating IT deeply into every function, breaking down silos, and fostering innovation.

Conway's Law reminds us that the structure and culture of an organization impacts the design of its technology systems. In a fusion organization, these challenges become opportunities. By rethinking our organizational structures and communication pathways, we stand a better chance of being able to plan for, and respond to, the technology changes ahead.

As strategy becomes more emergent and less directive, the guard rails of an enterprise purpose and culture, supported by modern leadership, become critical to success.

The application of the technologies and organizing principles discussed in this book take us a step closer to fully aligning how we build IT solutions with how we organize our businesses. We take Conway's Law to the next level by creating adaptable structures that evolve with changing needs, empowering teams with autonomy and decision-making capabilities to drive innovation and resilience.

Organizations are not frictionless, neither are human relations, and the software systems we build will always reflect this… despite AI.

# Technologies Fuelling Fusion Organizations

AI and machine learning are at the heart of this transformation, driving smarter decision-making and operational efficiency. Cloud computing provides the scalability and flexibility needed to support rapid innovation. APIs and big data enable seamless integration and data-driven insights, enabling organizations to make informed, strategic decisions.

# Leadership Transformation

In this new context, all executives must embrace their roles as digital leaders. The traditional boundaries between business and technology are dissolving, making it imperative for all leaders to understand and manage technology effectively.

Transformational leadership emphasizes that effectiveness in an AI-driven world requires a balance of qualities with intuition and spiritual awareness (SQ) being crucial for navigating rapid change, fostering innovation, and ensuring long-term organizational success.

In terms of strategic roles, the Chief Technology Officer, Enterprise Architect, Chief Information Security Officer and Customer Experience Designer are clearly in ascent. These roles are pivotal to creating the innovative, autonomous, resilient and integrated systems that define modern organizations.

# Cybersecurity

Security by design is non-negotiable. As we integrate new technologies, we must also embed robust cybersecurity measures to protect our data and operations. Effective risk management strategies help to navigate the complexities of digital transformation and ensure compliance with evolving regulations.

# The Human Element

People and culture are at the core of any successful transformation. Preparing the workforce, at all levels, for the future involves fostering a culture of continuous learning and adaptability. Ethical considerations and governance frameworks are vital to guide the responsible use of AI and other technologies, ensuring that they benefit all stakeholders – including society and the planet.

We must balance rapid innovation with organizational stability, ensuring that our systems are both flexible and robust.

Leaders must embody the qualities necessary to guide their organizations through these transformative times, building the right culture for the organization.

## What's Next?

The future of AI and digital transformation is full of promise, and technology will continue to confront, challenge, shape and reshape our organizations.

It's hard to know what happens next, but one thing is certain: not much of the future will be a linear extrapolation of the past. We must determine our own paths through uncertainty and ambiguity and make new footprints in the sands of time.

# Appendix

A Selection of Tech Jargon, Terminology,
Acronyms, and Abbreviations

# A

**Algorithm:** a process or set of rules to be followed in calculations or other problem-solving operations.

**API (application programming interface):** a set of protocols and tools for building and interacting with software applications.

**Application server:** a server that hosts and runs specific applications for users.

**Artificial neural network:** a computing system inspired by the biological neural networks that constitute animal brains.

# B

**Backlog:** a prioritized list of tasks and features to be developed.

**Backpropagation:** a method used to train artificial neural networks by adjusting the network's internal parameters to improve its performance.

**BI (business intelligence):** technologies and strategies used for data analysis and business information management.

**Big data:** extremely large datasets analysed computationally to reveal patterns, trends, and associations.

**Blockchain:** a decentralized ledger of all transactions in a network.

# C

**CDN (content delivery network):** a network of servers delivering web content to users based on geographic location.

**CI/CD (continuous integration/continuous delivery):** practices involving automatically testing and deploying code changes.

**Cloud computing:** delivery of computing services over the internet, including storage, processing, and software.

**Container:** a lightweight, stand-alone package that includes everything needed to run a piece of software.

**CRM (customer relationship management):** technology for managing a company's relationships and interactions with customers.

**Cybersecurity:** the practice of protecting systems, networks, and programs from digital attacks.

**C#:** a language developed by Microsoft, integral to the .NET framework, widely used for building Windows applications.

# D

**Data lake:** a storage repository holding vast amounts of raw data in its native format.

**Data lakehouse:** combination of data lake and data warehouse.

**Data mining:** the process of discovering patterns and knowledge from large amounts of data.

**Data science:** an interdisciplinary field using scientific methods to extract knowledge from data.

**Data warehouse:** a centralized repository for storing large volumes of structured data.

**DDoS (Distributed Denial of Service) attack:** a malicious attempt to disrupt the normal traffic of a targeted server, service, or network.

**DevOps:** practices combining software development (Dev) and IT operations (Ops) to shorten the development life cycle.

# E

**Edge computing:** processing data closer to where it is generated to reduce latency and bandwidth use.

**ERP (enterprise resource planning):** integrated management of main business processes, often in real time.

# F

**Firewall:** a network security system monitoring and controlling incoming and outgoing network traffic.

**Front end:** the client side of web applications involving everything users interact with directly.

# G

**GAN (generative adversarial network):** a class of machine learning frameworks designed by two neural networks competing against each other.

**GUI (graphical user interface):** a user interface including graphical elements like windows, icons, and buttons.

# H

**Hypervisor:** software creating and running virtual machines by separating physical hardware from the operating system.

# I

**IaaS (infrastructure as a service):** provides virtualized computing resources over the internet.

**IAM (identity and access management):** a framework for managing digital identities and access to resources.

**Inference:** the process whereby a pre-trained AI model applies its learned knowledge to new data in order to make predictions, generate insights, or perform specific tasks.

**IoT (internet of things):** the network of physical objects embedded with sensors and software to connect and exchange data.

**IP (internet protocol):** the principal communications protocol for relaying datagrams across network boundaries.

# J

**Java:** a high-level, class-based, object-oriented programming language.

**JavaScript:** a programming language commonly used to create interactive effects within web browsers. The backbone of web development.

**JSON (JavaScript Object Notation):** a lightweight data-interchange format easy for humans to read and write, and for machines to parse and generate.

# K

**Kubernetes:** an open-source platform automating deploying, scaling, and operating application containers.

# L

**LAN (local area network):** a network connecting computers within a limited area.

**Load balancer:** a device distributing network or application traffic across multiple servers.

**Load testing:** the process of putting demand on a system and measuring its response.

# M

**Machine learning:** a type of AI enabling a system to learn from data rather than through explicit programming.

**MFA (multi-factor authentication):** a security system requiring more than one method of authentication to verify the user's identity.

**Microservices:** an architectural style structuring an application as a collection of small, autonomous services.

# N

**NAT (network address translation):** a method of remapping one IP address space into another by modifying network address information.

**NLP (Natural Language Processing):** a branch of AI that enables systems to understand, interpret, and generate human language.

**NoSQL:** a class of database management systems not using a traditional relational database schema.

# O

**OAuth (open authorization):** an open standard for access delegation, commonly used for allowing access without sharing a password.

**Open source:** software with source code that anyone can inspect, modify, and enhance.

# P

**PaaS (platform as a service):** provides a platform allowing customers to develop, run, and manage applications without dealing with underlying infrastructure.

**Patch management:** the process of distributing and applying updates to software.

**Penetration testing:** a simulated cyberattack against a computer system to check for exploitable vulnerabilities.

**Phishing:** a method of trying to gather personal information using deceptive emails and websites.

**Python:** a versatile language, beginner-friendly, widely used in web development, data science and AI.

# Q

**QoS (quality of service):** the description or measurement of the overall performance of a service.

# R

**Ransomware:** a type of malicious software designed to block access to a computer system until a sum of money is paid.

**Reinforcement learning:** an area of machine learning where an AI system learns from feedback to maximize some notion of a cumulative reward.

**REST (representational state transfer):** an architectural style for designing networked applications using stateless, client-server communication.

# S

**SaaS (software as a service):** delivers software applications over the internet on a subscription basis.

**Scrum:** an agile framework for managing complex knowledge work, especially software development.

**SDK (software development kit):** a collection of software development tools in one installable package.

**Serverless computing:** a cloud computing model where the cloud provider runs the server and manages resource allocation.

**SQL (structured query language):** a standardized programming language for managing relational databases.

**SSO (single sign-on):** an authentication process allowing a user to access multiple applications with one set of login credentials.

# T

**TCP/IP (transmission control protocol/internet protocol):** the suite of communications protocols used to connect hosts on the internet.

**Tokenization:** the process of protecting sensitive data by replacing it with an algorithmically generated number called a token.

# U

**UI (user interface):** the space where interactions between humans and machines occur.

**UX (user experience):** a person's emotions and attitudes about using a particular product, system, or service.

# V

**VLAN (virtual local area network):** a logical subgroup within a local area network configured to communicate as if they were attached to the same wire.

**VM (virtual machine):** an emulation of a physical computer providing the functionality of a physical computer.

**VPN (virtual private network):** a service encrypting internet traffic and protecting online identity.

# W

**WAF (web application firewall):** a firewall monitoring, filtering, and blocking data packets travelling to and from a web application.

**Webhooks:** an approach for handling events across web applications.

# X

**XML (extensible markup language):** a markup language defining a set of rules for encoding documents in a format both human-readable and machine-readable.

# Y

**YAML (YAML Ain't Markup Language):** a human-readable data standard used to write system configuration files.

# Z

**Zero trust:** a security concept where organizations should verify everything trying to connect to their systems.

# References and Notes

1   McKinsey, *The Case for Digital Reinvention,* 2017, **https://www.mckinsey.com/ capabilities/mckinsey-digital/our-insights/the-case-for-digital-reinvention** – retrieved March 2024.

2   Christopher Martlew, *Leadership Recharged!,* Troubador Publishing, 2004.

3   Christopher Martlew, *Changing the Mind of the Organization: Building Agile Teams,* Troubador Publishing, 2015.

4   Richard Dobbs, James Manyika, and Jonathan Woetzel, *No Ordinary Disruption: The Four Global Forces Breaking All the Trends*, New York, NY: Public Affairs, 2016.

5   It was Fred Brooks who coined the term Conway's Law in the visionary (and ever-relevant) IT handbook, *The Mythical Man-Month*, **http://www.melconway. com/Home/Conways_Law.html.**

6   Jurgen Appelo, *Agile Is Not Dying; It's Dissolving*, March 2024, **https:// www.linkedin.com/pulse/agile-dying-its-dissolving-jurgen-appelo-f9are/** – retrieved March 2024.

7   Tim Fountaine et al, *Getting AI to Scale*, Harvard Business Review, May-June 2021, **https://hbr.org/2021/05/getting-ai-to-scale** – retrieved March 2024.

8   Tim Sullivan, *Blitzscaling*, Harvard Business Review, April 2016, **https://hbr. org/2016/04/blitzscaling** – retrieved March 2024.

9   John McCarthy, Marvin L. Minsky, Nathaniel Rochester, and Claude E. Shannon., *A Proposal for the Dartmouth Summer Research Project on Artificial Intelligence,* **https://ojs.aaai.org/aimagazine/index.php/aimagazine/article/view/1904/1802.**

10  Boston Dynamics Agile Robot, Spot, **https://bostondynamics.com/products/ spot/** – retrieved June 2024.

11  Mark Wilson, *Walmart's AI-powered Store of the future is nothing like Amazon Go*, Fast Company, April 2019: **https://www.fastcompany.com/90340364/walmarts-ai- powered-store-of-the-future-is-nothing-like-amazon-go** – retrieved March 2024.

12  Vaswani et al, *Attention Is All You Need*, 2017, **https://proceedings.neurips.cc/ paper/2017/file/3f5ee243547dee91fbd053c1c4a845aa-Paper.pdf.**

13  ImageNet project is a large visual database designed for use in visual object recognition software research, **https://en.wikipedia.org/wiki/ImageNet .**

14  *The NHS Long Term Plan*, August 2019, **https://www.longtermplan.nhs.uk/ publication/nhs-long-term-plan/** – retrieved March 2024.

15  *Avanade AI Readiness Report,* **https://edge.sitecorecloud.io/avanadeinc2- dotcom-prod-19a8/media/project/avanade/avanade/assets/research/ generative-ai-readiness-report.pdf** – retrieved March 2024.

16  Sam Altman and Reid Hoffman, *AI for the Next Era* via YouTube, **https://www. youtube.com/watch?v=WHoWGNQRXb0** – retrieved March 2024.

17  Iain McGilchrist, *The Master and His Emissary – The Divided Brain and the Making of the Western World,* Yale University Press, 2019.

18  Thomas Pikkety, *Capital in the Twenty-First Century*, Harvard University Press, 2014,

19  Charles Handy, *The Age of Unreason*, Arrow Books Ltd., 1991.

20  *State of Cloud 2023*, Pluralsight, 2023: **https://learn.pluralsight.com/resource/ offers/2023/state-of-Cloud** – retrieved March 2024.

21  Bloomberg interview with *Nvidia* CEO, Jensen Huang, 29 August 2024, **https:// youtu.be/NC5NZPrxbHk**

22  Canva Chooses AWS to Support SS Million Global Users, 2019, **https://aws. amazon.com/solutions/case-studies/canva-2019/.**

23  *A History of Spotify's Journey to the Cloud,* 2019: **https://engineering.atspotify. com/2019/12/views-from-the-cloud-a-history-of-spotifys-journey-to-the- cloud-part-1-2/.**

24  *Lessons from Capital One's Cloud Migration Journey*, May 2024, **https://www. capitalone.com/software/blog/Cloud-migration-journey/.**

25  *The API Mandate: How a mythical memo from Jeff Bezos changed software forever*, https://konghq.com/blog/enterprise/api-mandate – retrieved March 2024.

26  Bosch corporate website, *Allow me, the AI Analytics Platform*, undated, https://www.bosch.com/stories/ai-in-manufacturing/ – retrieved April 2024.

27  Interview with Jensen Huang, Founder and CEO NVIDIA at Stanford Graduate School of Business 2024, https://youtu.be/IXLBTBBil2U?si=4H5IZbviYpPdTXUz.

28  By Splunk (a CISCO company) at https://www.splunk.com/en_us/form/ciso-report.html – retrieved March 2024.

29  My typology here was informed in part by C.G. Jung's types. Daniel D. Ofman proposes four "core quadrants" of personality in *Core Qualities: A Gateway to Human Resources,* Scriptum Publishers, 2002, which informed my approach to the CTO leadership analysis.

Professor Manfred Kets De Vries identifies three orientations in his analysis of power in *Organizational Paradoxes: Clinical Approaches To Management,* Routledge, 1995. The "networker", "chairman" and "banker" are based on his characterizations. I've added the "professional" to complete my selection.

Also inspired by *The Gods of Management* by Charles Handy, Business Books Limited, 1995.

30  Nicole Forsgren et al, *Accelerate: Building and Scaling High Performing Technology Organizations*, IT Revolution Press, 2018.

31  Jon R. Katzenbach & Douglas K. Smith, *The Wisdom of Teams*, McGraw Hill. Original copyright McKinsey & Company Inc., 1993.

32  Thomas J. Peters and Robert H. Waterman Jr, *In Search Of Excellence*, Harper & Rowe, 1982.

33  This was the first book I read on software engineering – in fact it was probably the first book ever written for a larger audience on the subject. First published in 1975, Frederick P. Brooks Jr.'s, *The Mythical Man-Month* (Addison-Wesley) remains largely valid today.

34  Nicole Forsgren et al, *Accelerate: Building and Scaling High Performing Technology Organizations*, IT Revolution Press, 2018.

35  I was trained by Dr Jeff Sutherland in Scrum in 2010. Jeff Sutherland created the first Scrum team in 1993 and worked with Ken Schwaber to formalise Scrum at OOPSLA '95 (a software engineering conference). Together, they extended and enhanced Scrum at many software companies, helped write the Agile Manifesto in 2001, available at **https://agilemanifesto.org/** – retrieved April 2024.

36  Ikujiro Nonaka and Hirotaka Takeuchi, *The New Product Development Game*, Harvard Business Review, 1986.

37  Jeffrey Liker, *The Toyota Way: 14 Management Principles from the World's Greatest Manufacturer*, McGraw Hill, 2003.

38  The Scaled Agile Framework (SAFe) provides a blueprint for large enterprises to adopt lean and agile methodologies effectively across their broader organization. It's part of a suite of frameworks, including Disciplined Agile Delivery (DAD) and Scrum@Scale (S@S), designed to tackle the unique challenges that surface when agile practices are expanded beyond the confines of a single team. These frameworks are becoming increasingly popular as more organizations seek agile solutions that can operate at scale. **https://scaledagileframework.com/**.

39  Paper written by the cognitive psychologist George A. Miller of Harvard University's Department of Psychology and published in 1956 in Psychological Review. Wikipedia summary: **https://en.wikipedia.org/wiki/The_Magical_Number_Seven,_Plus_or_Minus_Two**

40  Matthew Skelton and Manuel Pais, *Team Topologies – Organizing Business and Technology Teams for Fast Flow*, IT Revolution Press, 2019.

41  "Validated Learning" is a term proposed by Eric Ries in *The Lean Startup*, Penguin Random House LLC, 2011.

42  Based on Marty Cagan's (rather wordy, but very solid) definition in his book, *Inspired – How to Create Tech Products Customers Love*, Wiley, 2018.

43  Press release by Klarna, February 2024, **https://www.klarna.com/international/press/klarna-ai-assistant-handles-two-thirds-of-customer-service-chats-in-its-first-month/** – retrieved April 2024.

44  *Inside Tesla's Crazy AI Manufacturing Revolution,* March 2021, **https://streetfins.com/inside-teslas-crazy-ai-manufacturing-revolution/** – retrieved March 2024.

45  *10 Examples Of Predictive Customer Experience Outcomes Powered By AI,* Forbes magazine, December 2018, **https://www.forbes.com/sites/blakemorgan/2018/12/20/10-examples-of-predictive-customer-experience-outcomes-powered-by-ai/** – retrieved March 2024.

46  *How Amazon Fashion is using Ai to help you find the perfect fit,* January 2024: **https://www.aboutamazon.com/news/retail/how-amazon-is-using-ai-to-help-customers-shop** – retrieved February 2024.

47  X (Twitter) developer blog, November 2021: https:**//developer.twitter.com/en/blog/product-news/2021/three-approaches-to-topic-discovery-with-x-data** – retrieved May 2024.

48  The Renzo Piano Building Workshop (RPBW) creates some of the world's most spectacular buildings. **https://www.rpbw.com/story/philosophy-of-rpbw**.

49  Dr Rasmussen, Steen Eiler, *Experiencing Architecture,* 1959.

50  Article in Dutch magazine *IT Executive,* September 2022, **https://itexecutive.nl/architectuur/rabobank-een-verfrissende-kijk-op-architectuur/** – retrieved April 2024.

51  The Open Group Architecture Framework: **https://pubs.opengroup.org/architecture/togaf9-doc/arch/**.

52  E.F. Schumacher, *Small is Beautiful: A Study of Economics as if People Mattered,* Blond & Briggs and HarperCollins, 1973–present.

53  CSO magazine, April 2024: **https://www.csoonline.com/article/567531/the-biggest-data-breach-fines-penalties-and-settlements-so-far.html** – retrieved April 2024.

54   Duo.com, September 2020:   **https://duo.com/decipher/gartner-warns-ceos-will-be-personally-liable-for-breaches-by-2024** – retrieved April 2024.

55   **https://e-estonia.com/** for excellent background on Estonia's journey to becoming the world's most advanced digital society.

56   BBC report, April 2017, *How a cyber attack transformed Estonia*, **BBC News.**

57   UK government press release, *Russia behind a cyber attack before Ukraine invasion*, May 2022: **https://www.gov.uk/government/news/russia-behind-cyber-attack-with-europe-wide-impact-an-hour-before-ukraine-invasion.**

58   Microsoft actions following an attack by a nation state actor: Microsoft blog, January 2024. **https://msrc.microsoft.com/blog/2024/01/microsoft-actions-following-attack-by-nation-state-actor-midnight-blizzard/.**

59   **Wikipedia on the CrowdStrike incident, https://en.wikipedia.org/wiki/2024_CrowdStrike_incident** – retrieved August 2024

60   VentureBeat, February 2023, **https://venturebeat.com/security/benchmarking-your-cybersecurity-budget-in-2023/** – retrieved April 2024.

61   Deloitte, *Cybersecurity insights 2023: Budgets and benchmarks for financial services institutions*, 2023, **https://www.deloitte.com/global/en/services/risk-advisory/perspectives/cybersecurity-insights-budgets-benchmarks-financial-services-institutions.html** – retrieved May 2024.

62   The CISO Report by Splunk, undated: **https://www.splunk.com/en_us/pdfs/gated/ebooks/the-ciso-report.pdf** – retrieved April 2024.

63   Deloitte Insights report, December 2021: **https://www.deloitte.com/lv/en/our-thinking/insights/topics/technology-management/tech-trends/2022/future-of-cybersecurity-and-ai.html** – retrieved March 2024.

64   CISO Magazine, September 2020: **https://cisomag.com/psychology-of-human-error-could-help-businesses-prevent-security-breaches/** – retrieved March 2024.

65   Daniel Goleman, *The New Leaders*, Little, Brown, 2002.

66   The Verge, November 2022, **https://www.theverge.com/2022/11/28/23481786/ meta-fine-facebook-data-leak-ireland-dpc-gdpr**

67   European Data Protection Board, May 2023:   **https://www.edpb.europa.eu/ news/news/2023/12-billion-euro-fine-facebook-result-edpb-binding-decision_ en**  – retrieved March 2024.

# ACKNOWLEDGEMENTS

Writing is fundamentally a solitary craft, but there were a number of people who contributed directly or indirectly to the emergence of this book, and I'm very grateful to them all.

I'd particularly like to thank Dr David Walker, Nicolas Castellon, Padraig O'Riordain, Frank Boekel, Vincent Verpoort and Joseph Souren for going through early versions of the manuscript and offering feedback that has materially improved the book.

Special thanks to Michael Tobin for the foreword and to Brian Bacon for his encouragement along the way.

Thanks also to the great team at Troubador, with whom I've worked now for the third time.

As always, the buck stops here, and any and all mistakes are solely my responsibility.

Many thanks,
Christopher Martlew

# ABOUT THE AUTHOR

Christopher Martlew has worked in the technology industry for over three decades. He's been a "digital executive" with start-ups, scale-ups, and multinational corporations.

His career spans the technology, e-commerce, and fintech sectors, where he has successfully built high-growth businesses and navigated several mergers and acquisitions. Christopher is the founder of Tangible Management Services, providing non-executive, consulting, and management services to clients.

He writes and speaks about leadership, technology, and organizational change. His previous titles, *Changing the Mind of the Organization* and *Leadership Recharged*, explored these areas. This is his third book. He also contributes regularly through his online blog and on LinkedIn.

Initially trained in computer science, he holds an MBA from Kingston University London and is a fellow of the RSA.

#onbeingagile

www.ingramcontent.com/pod-product-compliance
Lightning Source LLC
LaVergne TN
LVHW011803070326
832902LV00026B/4619